The Myth of the Unt Therapist

Therapists are often expected to be immune to the kind of problems that they help clients through. This book serves to demonstrate that this is certainly not the case: they are no more resistant to difficult and unexpected personal circumstances than anyone else. In this book Marie Adams looks into the kind of problems that therapists can be afraid to face in their own lives, including divorce, bereavement, illness, depression and anxiety, and uses the experience of others to examine the best ways of dealing with them.

The Myth of the Untroubled Therapist looks at the lives of forty practitioners to learn how they coped during times of personal strife. CBT, psychoanalytic, integrative and humanistic therapists from an international array of backgrounds were interviewed about how they believed their personal lives affected their work with clients. Over half admitted to suffering from depression since entering the profession and many continued practising while ill or under great stress. Some admitted to using their work as a 'buffer' against their personal circumstances in an attempt to avoid focusing on their own pain. Using clinical examples, personal experience, research literature and the voices of the many therapists interviewed, Adams challenges mental health professionals to take a step back and consider their own well-being as a vital first step to promoting insight and change in those they seek to help.

Linking therapists' personal histories to their choice of career, *The Myth of the Untroubled Therapist* pinpoints some of the key elements that may serve, and sometimes undermine, counsellors working in private practice or mental health settings. The book is ideal for counsellors and psychotherapists as well as social workers and those working within any kind of helping profession.

Marie Adams is a psychotherapist and writer. Along with her private practice she teaches on the DPsych programme at the Metanoia Institute in London. She is also a consultant psychotherapist for the BBC, leading workshops for journalists and production staff on trauma and mental health.

The Myth of the Untroubled Therapist

Private life, professional practice

Marie Adams

Routledge
Taylor & Francis Group

LONDON AND NEW YORK

First published 2014
by Routledge
27 Church Road, Hove, East Sussex BN3 2FA

and by Routledge
711 Third Avenue, New York, NY 10017

Routledge is an imprint of the Taylor & Francis Group, an informa business

British Library Cataloguing in Publication Data
A catalogue record for this book is available from the British Library

Library of Congress Cataloging in Publication Data
Adams, Marie (Psychotherapist)
The myth of the untroubled therapist : private life, professional practice / Marie Adams.
    pages cm
    1. Psychotherapists – Mental health – Case studies. 2. Psychotherapy – Practice – Psychological aspects. 3. Depression, Mental. I. Title.
    RC451.4.P79A33 2013
    616.89'14–dc23   2013018758

ISBN: 978-0-415-53259-4 (hbk)
ISBN: 978-0-415-53260-0 (pbk)
ISBN: 978-1-315-88016-7 (ebk)

Typeset in Times
by HWA Text and Data Management, London

Contents

Acknowledgements

With deep gratitude to the forty therapists who took part in this research project, for their courage and their openness.

To Donald Freed, for paving the way and never letting me forget the writer's 'debt of honour'. I owe him more than I can say.

To David Mann and Alistair McBeath, for their constant support and productive feedback.

To Dorrit Breitenstein, Susi Noble and Ros Pines, who bore the early brunt of my research interest.

To Brigitte Weusten, who has never let distance interfere with the quality of her support and encouragement.

To Professor Richard Gerberding who once said, 'Adams, there are a thousand and three things I'd rather do than teach you anything', but learn from him I did!

To Laura Stobart, Victoria Jones, Richard Bath, Tilly Lavernas, Patricia Rae Freed and Rosie Allsop, for holding true and keeping me steady.

And to Gordon, who contributes so much to the personal life of this therapist and without whom my life would be greatly diminished.

Introduction

Several years after qualifying as a psychotherapist, I faced a professional complaint. It was eventually dropped, but only after five months of stratospheric anxiety. Eighteen months later I was cycling up the hill towards my therapist's office for my regular, early morning appointment. Walking down the hill was my former client. Terrified, as if she had magic powers to destroy me, I huffed and puffed my way past her. I was decked out in a bicycle helmet and the meeting was so unlikely she probably did not recognise me. Who knows? Sometimes I had experienced visions of her stalking me, though these had passed with time, and I had little evidence other than the occasional silent phone call.

A few minutes later in therapy I revisited again the pain of the complaint, recalling the nightmare of those months when I believed my career was in such jeopardy. When the session was over, back out I went, this time cycling down the hill. At the very spot where I had seen my former client just an hour before, I fell off my bike, nearly killing myself in the traffic.

So, the complaint was gone, but not forgotten, some destructive energy inside me still, the unconscious legacy of a trauma I thought I had left behind. Working as a psychotherapist is difficult. But facing myself is harder still, and facing myself *in relation* to my clients the most painful task of all. This book, and the research behind it, is the legacy from this difficult period in my life, a time when I felt both personally and professionally threatened.

The research: a personal investment

This book is largely the product of doctoral research into the personal lives of forty therapists, and the resulting challenges in their clinical work. Professional discussions, observations and friendly chats with colleagues have also contributed to my thinking, forcing me to consider more deeply my own life and the impact this has on my practice. I cannot write about the personal lives of therapists without in some way revealing aspects of my own.

I embarked on research to determine how therapists' personal lives affected their practice because I knew with certainty that it had impacted mine during at least two crucial periods of my life – the first when my husband was very ill, and the second when facing that professional complaint. My husband recovered and the complaint was dropped, but not before I had experienced intense anxiety and, in the second case, the addition of profound shame.

How was I as a therapist during these crises? I found working a relief from my worries about my husband, and to some degree I was present and active in my therapeutic relationships. Like many of the therapists I spoke to, my capacity for empathy may even have been heightened. But I was also very tired from lack of sleep and I was always on the lookout for unusual sounds in the house, in case there was an emergency. I couldn't possibly have been all there for my clients.

During the period of the complaint, my practice was more likely directly impacted. When it was all over, one of my supervisees said, 'I knew something was wrong, I just didn't know what.' So much for bracketing then.

I am now convinced that this wonderful term 'bracketing' is simply an illusion, a comforting idea that bears no relation to reality. We *cannot* leave our experiences outside the room. Even if not at the foreground of our minds, our tensions and pleasures, the rumbling envies and unresolved issues of archaic experience, are always with us.

Fear and shame were the primary conscious feelings I carried with me throughout the period when the complaint was active. How had I got into this mess? And what would happen to me if I was found at fault? I was also furious. How could this complaint possibly be taken so seriously? Couldn't they *see* that this was all an enactment of my former client's appalling history?

Eventually the complaint was dropped and during the ensuing months my life began to take on a more familiar pattern. I was able to write again, enjoy a novel and go to the movies for enjoyment rather than distraction, and hiking and running were opportunities for thinking things through rather than ruminating endlessly on a repetitive loop concerning an imagined, catastrophic future.

But there was also a legacy, perhaps a little less hubris but also the sliver of an idea that I had in some way contributed to the complaint, no matter how unjustified it was on the surface. I was forced to look at myself, an unnerving process if there ever was one (Adams, 2008).

There have been other life events as well, of course, and bad days that drop like a brick when things aren't necessarily going my way. I have moved, opened a new practice and taken on different academic responsibilities that sometimes interfere with my clinical schedule. I have colds, sore knees and worries about my ageing father back in Canada. I have pleasures and disappointments, pre-occupations and wishes that sometimes don't come true. In other words, I am entirely human, and I bring with me every single day into the therapy room a wealth of imperfections. How I use my humanity is up to me, hopefully in the service of my clients, but sometimes it is bound to interfere. Like most people, I sometimes want to be seen as better than I am.

Purpose of the book

During that difficult period facing the complaint, I was open about my predicament – not concerning the details of the case, but about the distress it evoked in me. I did this, not through wisdom, but rather because I knew that if I kept it to myself it would become a 'dirty' little secret. I needed help, and I received it in spades, from family and friends and, most importantly under these circumstances, from colleagues. They also began to tell me about their own difficulties while working, including relationship problems, struggles with depression and anxiety and the haunting by old ghosts from their past when working with particular clients. None of us, it seems, is ever completely untroubled, no matter how extensive our experience of personal therapy or solid our relationships. Life happens and, as Yalom points out, 'there is no therapist and no person immune to the inherent tragedies of existence' (2002, p. 8). What is important, however, is how we manage our struggles, particularly in the context of our work as therapists. And the more we know of how other therapists faced difficulties, how they might choose to do things differently next time, or what was positive about the way they tackled their personal crisis, the better equipped we may be to manage our own. If, like Casement, we can 'learn' from our patients (Casement, 1985, 1990), we can certainly also learn from one another.

I hope that by highlighting other therapists' stories of pain and personal trauma, this will help experienced clinicians re-evaluate their personal lives in view of their practice. For those just entering the field, either still studying or recently qualified, perhaps they can take heart from knowing that *every* therapist has a back story, as well as an evolving narrative that can often work in the service of their clients, but sometimes may also stand in the way. The challenge is not to delude ourselves that we are able to leave our tensions at the door. Life happens, regardless of how conscientious or committed a therapist we might be.

For those who are interested in entering the field of counselling and psychotherapy, perhaps tales of personal struggle will be enlightening, even making it less frightening for those considering entering therapy for the first time. And teachers, social workers, care workers, priests and ministers, physicians, even lawyers, all those professionals who deal every day with the lives of others, might find some resonance here regarding their responses to particular students, clients or patients, and some recognition that their choice of profession was *never* an accident of circumstances.

This book is not intended to be a comprehensive study of any one area of therapeutic practice. It simply highlights some of the areas where we might be vulnerable. It is up to each of us to explore further those aspects of pain and personal crisis, joy and enlightenment that may be worth delving into more deeply, through further reading or personal therapy. The work, quite frankly, never ends.

Conducting the research

The formal aspect of my doctoral research included interviewing forty psychotherapists across the UK, Australia and Canada. I broke them down equally into four broad traditions: psychoanalytic, humanistic, integrative and cognitive/behavioural (CBT). I wanted to know if they believed that their personal lives affected their work (they all did) and in which way. Had they ever been depressed since working as a therapist? Had they taken time off during times of crisis, and what kind of support had they received? What was the significant event in their lives that had led them to becoming a therapist, and what was it that led them to become the *kind* of therapist they were now?

The interviews usually lasted an hour. Most were interviewed in or near their place of work. One therapist chose to visit my office and another to be interviewed in a cafe. Another visited me in my hotel suite as they worked outside the city I was visiting at the time. In addition, friends and colleagues also granted me permission to make use of their material, for which I am deeply grateful.

Outline of the book

The text can be read sequentially, though each chapter stands on its own, focusing on a particular aspect of experience in the lives of therapists. Following on from the first chapter, highlighting the 'myth' of the untroubled therapist, the second chapter discusses the impact parenthood has on many therapists, while also looking at some of the pressures being a therapist puts on families. And what does it mean *not* to have children, what issues of envy, or inadequacy, might this evoke in some therapists, particularly when working with pregnant clients?

Chapter 3 is concerned with the issue of physical pain in the lives of therapists, often replicating the psychic pain of those they work with, but also sometimes diminishing their ability to attend to their patients as deeply as they would like.

In Chapter 4, the high rate of depression amongst therapists is considered, while Chapter 5 looks at the impact of the clinician's anxiety on their work within the therapeutic space.

Chapter 6 brings us to therapists' histories and how this so obviously determined not only their choice of profession, but also the model in which they chose to train.

In Chapter 7, there is a focus on home life in general and the sometimes tricky issues of money, the pressures that being a therapist can put on a relationship, and the need to maintain a professional profile within a community while also feeling the need to withhold evidence of personal domestic struggles. Chapter 8 considers illness, and death within the family.

Chapter 9 is concerned with the need to maintain good professional links, maintain supervision and develop a 'community' of therapists to pin us to the ground when the temptation to fly too close to the sun becomes overwhelming. In Chapter 10, I revisit some of the earlier themes, finally letting go of the 'myth' of the untroubled therapist. My belief is that our essential quality, and the most important gift we can give our clients and patients, is our humanity, our feet firmly on the ground.

Throughout the book I have used the words 'client' and 'patient' interchangeably, as I have 'therapist' and 'psychotherapist'. I have noted the therapeutic tradition within which they work only when I believe it is relevant. All names are pseudonyms and I have gone to considerable lengths to hide identities.

Research: more questions than answers

This book is not so much about the results of my research as it is about the questions it raised. From the beginning, my inquiry was intended to develop areas for discussion, rather than to prove a point. Like our clients, every therapist has their own story to tell, and how they deal with difficult personal circumstances is as individual as the narrative surrounding it.

All of these therapists gave to the interview as best they could. I witnessed bravery, shame, grief and terrible stories of childhood abandonment. I was moved, irritated, impressed and shocked at various times. A few frightened me, but most were willing to consider the possibility of unconscious motives and worked with integrity. Shame, in my view, appeared to be the biggest hindrance to self-exploration, threatening as it does, our deepest sense of worth (Nathanson, 1987). Why would anyone want to venture where the terrain is so uncomfortable, and where for some of us it may even feel life threatening, at least on a psychic level?

Therapists have a 'current' life, but unlike most other professions, they have a responsibility to understand how unconscious processes can impact their relationships with others, particularly with clients and patients. Like physicians we have a duty to 'do no harm' at the very least, and to promote instead the psychological well-being of our clients. I argue that we can only do this through recognition of our own weaknesses and a willingness to understand how we might be tempted into positions of false omnipotence, moral superiority and boundary violations. This will be true no matter how big our intellect, and despite our deep capacity for empathy. Like Guggenbuhl-Craig, I believe there is a 'bogeyman' within every therapist, longing for control (1971, p. 55).

On the couch: personal experience

I have had three important therapists in my life. The first was a man who saved my life. I met him when I was sixteen, an unhappy teenager toying with notions of suicide. The second I saw during my early years of training, and the third I attended regularly during my post-graduate studying and beyond. All three of these therapists were distinguished by their humanity.

There were other therapists along the way. One of them I saw for several months because I was so desperate at the time that I would have remained with anyone who stayed put in a chair and appeared to listen, which is the sum total of what he accomplished. I'm not sure that he was ever capable of actually *hearing* me; he was so busy asking me to change my appointment times because he had tickets to Wimbledon, or some other sporting or cultural event. A little too slick, a little too well dressed, he positively glowed in his chair. And he was a bit too quick with his interventions, his face settling into a self-satisfied grin after every clever 'interpretation'. I don't imagine he was a bad guy, but he didn't have the *essence* that made the others so particularly good at what they did, at least with me.

I have tried over the years to determine how it was that these three therapists managed to convey their humanity, and their qualities of humility, even while I knew so little about them.

About Dr K, my first therapist, I knew absolutely nothing, other than that he was obviously Jewish, loved Hawaii and for a time had worked with adolescents in New York City. He was a storyteller, which I believe now was his particularly canny way of responding to my own need to place myself within a narrative context. Many years later, I also recognise that he had his own story too, one that at the very least involved the tragedy of his generation, that of the Holocaust. He once told of a rooftop sniper, who narrowly missed killing his friend. Walking along the path, he happened to look up at the crucial moment, giving him time to take cover. Life is a crap shoot, Dr K seemed to be telling me, and sometimes it hangs by a thread. You can live, and still make a point.

He suggested I read certain books, *The Other America* (Harrington, 1998), focusing on America's underclass in the 1960s, and *Manchild in The Promised Land* (Brown, 2000), the story of a survivor of the New York City ghetto, both of which gave me a window into another world, into other people's despair. Perhaps he recognised something of my own emotional impoverishment, or he could see a willingness in me to try and make sense of the world. Regardless, he opened up a crack in my own wall of pain and allowed me to see through it into the ravaged hurt of others' lives. As I said, he saved my life, and so many years later I believe that it was through his personal sensitivity to the precarious nature of life that he recognised the value of mine.

There was a broken marriage in the life of my second significant therapist and a much earlier suicide attempt on the part of the third, elements of personal tragedy that certainly contributed to sensitivity towards others within the therapy room. By this time I was nearing the end of my studies and, as so many of the therapists I have spoken to over the last few years have pointed out, the therapy world is a small one, and even over international borders, news travels. We may want to hide behind the shield of our professional persona, but that may be impossible, as likely to leak within the therapy room as it is over the channels of worldwide communication.

It is my contention that the very elements that these therapists brought to their work in that small room with me are often the very things that we feel as therapists should remain hidden. Sometimes we want to hide our vulnerability from ourselves, but certainly we do from our patients and colleagues. Perhaps we want to be seen as having conquered life's traumas, proving somehow that therapy works. If we can embody that success, we can prove to ourselves and others that what we do for a living has validity. We may want to look capable of empathy, but not worth empathising towards when it comes to our confusion, our sense of helplessness and the terrible determination of archaic experience to reawaken, rising up like the horrifying fist from the water in the film *Deliverance* (Boorman, 1972), 'pain that cannot forget' rising up even in our dreams.[1] This is particularly difficult when we thought we had it all sorted out previously.

Distrust and shame

Psychotherapists don't always appear to trust other therapists with their confidences. We have little faith that our human frailties will be valued rather than judged as proof that we should not be working. The very thing we aim to extend to our patients and clients, we often fear will not be extended towards us when facing depression, physical disability and pain, marital strife, alcoholism, a partner or child's mental illness, financial difficulties or any other emotional crisis that we may have to face in our lives.

As I witnessed so many times in the course of interviewing therapists, we often feel shame over the very vulnerability that I believe is essential in determining a great therapist and places us at a level with those with whom we work. No one is immune from the vagaries of life, it is simply how they are managed, how they are admitted, and how they are understood within the context of both our personal and our professional lives that makes or breaks us as therapists.

Conclusion

Every practitioner I spoke to in the course of researching this book was able to track his or her reason for becoming a therapist back to some wounding and meaningful aspect of their history. So why do so many therapists struggle at the possibility of taking help for themselves following their training? Why is there so much shame attached to those personal difficulties that are inevitable in life, regardless of the work we do? We are not *above* those we counsel, we are part of the great heaving mass of humanity that has to work and struggle, make a buck and sort out the difficulties in our family lives just like everyone else.

We face the pressure of the workplace in hard times, we have to feed and educate our children, we have to face widowhood and psychotic episodes in ourselves, our partners and those we love best in the world. We have to contend with addictions; the temptation to cross the line, both within our committed relationships and within our work; we need to pay our mortgages and find ways of having a life outside the confines of the therapy room, often the place we find most comfortable, and sometimes the safest and blessedly removed from the problems we face outside. Like those in other professions, we find solace in our work.

And we need job satisfaction, to see our clients and patients responding in their therapy and, due to what we can offer them, finding a way to manage their difficulties. But in our work, many of us have also found an unconscious method of self-medicating; helping to fix in others' lives what went so disastrously wrong in our own. How is it that the therapist who suffered the brunt of his sister's psychosis as an adolescent now works with teenagers the same age he was at the time, but refuses to work with psychosis? Like every professional engaged in a caring profession, we may work to help others, but our main, unconscious, objective may be to save ourselves.

I am not arguing that this is a bad thing, only that we may need to be conscious of it on a day-to-day level, rather than simply hold it in vague awareness and trust that it is always for the good. Sometimes it may also inhibit us as therapists, for instance in our assumptions of a patient's experience of depression or motherhood.

I am no exception, of course, and the route to my training as a therapist in my middle years I can connect directly back to the death of my sister when I was only eighteen months old. My mother, suffering the terrible grief of her lost child, found it difficult to deal with a toddler who at that age was full of the spirit of independence and self-discovery. I may have saved my grieving mother with my liveliness, as she always contended, but I had to enliven her too, and reckon with the idealised notions of the child she had lost, an image I couldn't possibly live up to. Perhaps this was also linked to my own ideation of suicide as a teenager – a dead child is a perfect child and I might finally win my mother's love.

But Dr K was brought in, and in his ability to tell a story, to acknowledge my anger and my longing for some acknowledgement of my vulnerability he made it possible for me to move into adulthood alive and full of the notion of life's possibilities. Those gifts he gave me have never left me. I was able to internalise him, because he was able to accept my projections and to make sense of them for me. He let me in, indicating a capacity for acceptance and reflection I believe only those therapists who are open to their own human frailty are able to do. These therapists are not gurus, nor are they relying solely on their clients and patients to give them a sense of worth. They are boundaried and provide containment, and it is my contention that this is achieved through an acceptance of their own fragility, through which they allow their clients and patients to accept their own.

Note

1 Aeschylus: Agamemnon

1 The untroubled therapist

Buying the myth

There are perhaps two questions here:

1 Why did you train to become a therapist?
2 Why did you *really* train to become a therapist?

The first is likely the story you gave the interviewing panel when first applying to become a counsellor/psychologist/psychotherapist. Not quite a 'myth', it isn't the real story either. Applying to join a training programme with rigorous standards of personal integrity, you are hardly likely to want to expose yourself too deeply. Nor is it appropriate to do so.

But the second question is the deeper, truer issue, often worked out in therapy, through long hours of battle with depression or internal demons. It is the drive behind how you behave, maintain, or struggle with relationships. Within these greater or lesser archaic traumas will rest the more profound truth of why you are training, or have become a therapist: the reason behind the reason, if you like, and the less 'pure' motivation for training as a therapist, echoing as it does an infantile deficit, or need. In every therapist there is also a client, as in every physician there is also a patient. To deny that equation is to deny the other, the very person whom we purport to want to help. And placing ourselves in a position of being the 'carer' rather than the one seeking help may help sustain the delusion that we are not in 'need'. Yalom says that during his training he was continually reminded of the idea of the 'fully analysed therapist' (2002, p. 8), a notion he recognises now cannot possibly be true. This would also, in my view, mean believing we live in a state of stasis, without movement or texture in our lives – a kind of emotional flat-lining.

Therapy is increasingly a prerequisite for training as a therapist – even CBT therapists and psychologists training in academic settings are now encouraged to avail themselves of psychotherapy for at least a short period.

As a trainer and examiner of psychotherapists, I am always concerned when I detect a resistance to engaging in any further therapy following training, as if therapeutic nirvana can be achieved through the attendance of so many hours. The truth is, we may need to revisit earlier trauma over and over again during our lives, each new decade perhaps bringing new elements to the fore. We see this in our clients: those who have suffered sexual abuse for instance, may find some peace through therapy in their twenties, but becoming a parent may raise new anxieties that must be contained and resolved a few years later. Why should this not be true with us, particularly as every day we work with the pain and trauma of others, some of which will echo our own life experiences? We can rise above it, of course, looking down on our clients from the dazzling height of our own delusions of perfection, or we can accept that we are sometimes troubled souls, with vulnerabilities of our own. A fair number of gurus may act as a warning.

The trouble with gurus

Gurus are a paradoxical lot. The very nature of being a guru is that you have followers, which lends itself to intense idealisation. And the higher up we are on the pedestal, the further the drop when we hit the ground. So why is it that there are those who aspire to such heady and precarious heights?

Most of us are not gurus, of course. We are working therapists, on the front line of the profession in private practice or within a mental health system. We work hard and juggle our professional lives against the backdrop of our personal lives, and mostly we manage. Gurus, however, seem to have a hard time of it. The effort of combining public scrutiny with human frailty seems to aggravate both into points of extreme.

R.D. Laing was perhaps the most influential psychiatrist during the 1960s and 1970s and even into the 1980s. That he changed people's perception of madness is an understatement. As a therapist he was certainly remarkable, if his public demonstrations are anything to go by: he notoriously stripped down naked to sit with an equally naked patient suffering psychosis. However, 'As a man Laing could be mean and cruel, especially to those close to him. But he clearly also had a remarkable ability to relate to people, men and women, in extreme states of suffering' (Gordon, 2009).

His own son writes, 'My relationship with Ronnie has greatly improved since his death' (Laing, 2006, p. xxi), making it clear in a single sentence that his father, the guru, was hardly an ideal parent. Laing's struggles with alcohol, relationships and his own fragile mental health are well documented (Barston, 1996; Gordon, 2009; Laing, 2006).

Perhaps less well known is the personal struggle faced by Scott Peck, the American psychiatrist and guru who wrote *The Road Less Travelled* (1978), which sat at the top of the *New York Times* best seller list long enough to warrant an entry in the *Guinness Book of World Records*. In America he sold seven million copies of the book and another three million worldwide. As Jones points out in his biography, by the time he died Peck was ostracised from his children and his wife of forty years had finally left him following years of alcohol and drug abuse and an endless series of affairs. 'His psychotherapeutic secret,' writes Jones, 'to the extent it was a secret, was that he knew what people yearned for, even when they didn't quite know themselves, because he yearned for it too. His skill was this ability to convey his understanding of their yearning in words that helped' (Jones, 2007, p. 9).

Eric Berne, the founder of transactional analysis, also struggled within his personal life. Although he redefined the word 'game' as a psychological metaphor (Berne, 1964), his biographers – both of them disciples – cannot escape the fact that he was a 'Master Gamesman' himself, unable to control his impulses or adhere to the very principles he established and to which so many people now aspire: to live an 'adult', game-free life (Jorgensen and Jorgensen, 1984).

I have mentioned only a few here, with very public profiles, but the list of leading therapists who showed evidence of human frailty, and who clung to their narcissistic perch rather than do anything about it, may be endless. Throughout the psychotherapeutic world, in big ponds and little ponds, there are countless gurus who head the pack and draw us in with their grace, wisdom and often their sublime confidence. Never doubt for a single moment that they are human too.

Beware the wounded healer?

Guy argues that 'the therapist's own pain may serve to motivate entry into the mental health field in the hopes of relieving similar pain in others' (1987, p. 15), but he goes on to warn:

> For those psychotherapists who continue in psychic distress, there may be the wish to share vicariously in the healing of others when personal relief seems unattainable. In such cases, the work of psychotherapy may take on a near messianic quality, as though personal relief will be achieved only when the gods are satisfied with the shaman's self-sacrifice and abnegation. (p. 15)

If we are drawn to particular aspects of practice, it is likely that even if we are effective in our work, dangers also lurk. Writing of 'development work', for instance, Renn (2012) points out that the therapist may feel 'legitimate' parental feelings towards the patient:

However, it needs to be acknowledged that there is a heightened countertransferential risk in developmental work of the therapist using the patient vicariously as a source of narcissistic gratification, to relieve guilt, to overcome feelings of helplessness or to gratify his or her own infantile needs. (p. 94)

Mair (1994) argues that psychotherapists 'exploit the mystique of the expert healer' suggesting that 'psychotherapy, like medicine, is said to be based on knowledge. Perhaps, like the medicine of eighty years ago, its true foundation is on the myth of knowledge' (p. 136). Therapy, she says, works because 'therapists deceive *themselves*' into believing that what they do has a scientific basis, and the patient believes them in turn, creating a form of 'placebo' effect (p. 167).

In his book *Against Therapy* (1989), Jeffrey Masson created a splash, outlining from his perspective the foibles of a number of well-known therapists including Jung, Freud, Ferenczi, Perls and Rogers. Interestingly, Masson grew up with a guru – his parents were in thrall to a 'mystic' who even lived for many years with the family in Los Angeles (Masson, 1993). Masson appears to have spent much of his early life alternating between idealisation and denigration: for a time he was even director of the Sigmund Freud archives.

A kind of anti-therapist guru himself, Masson is unforgiving in his approach. It is hard not to believe that he holds a grudge, perhaps sometimes driving those who think he has a point into a defensive position, for instance concerning the underlying motives for someone working as a psychotherapist. Claiming that many of us put the advancement of our career, or theoretical perspective, ahead of the welfare of our patients, he is 'sceptical of anybody who profits from another person's suffering' (Masson, 1989, p. 39).

'No one can act out of exclusively pure motives,' concurs Guggenbuhl-Craig, from a less damning position, 'Even the noblest deeds are based on pure and impure motives'. He further suggests that if a therapist deludes himself that his motives are selfless, he is more likely to act inappropriately within the consulting room (1971, p. 10).

Guggenbuhl-Craig writes from a Jungian perspective, focusing on the 'shadow' side of anyone entering the helping professions, including social workers, physicians and psychotherapists. How many times have I heard myself, as well as colleagues, refer to the nebulous 'shadow' in all of us? We pay verbal homage to ying and yang, the 'shadow side' and the notion of opposites, but in reality we may often avoid deeper consideration of the 'shadow' highlighting, as it does, uncomfortable aspects of the self. A well-established colleague of mine insists that therapy doesn't really begin until the therapist is through training. Until then, says my friend, the trainee more or less treads water, dipping occasionally but only as far as he thinks he can go safely without jeopardising his future as a therapist. He needs to be *seen* to be in good mental health. Stirring up the mud underneath is just a little too unsettling for most of us, exposing as it does the less noble side of ourselves.

On the other hand, the notion of 'pure and impure' rather reduces our internal complexity to good and bad, or black and white, like the cowboys of my childhood where all the bad guys invariably wore black Stetsons and the heroes always wore white. Our histories are what they are, and our motives for becoming therapists are rarely straightforward or simple. Out of consideration of the more distressing elements of our underlying motivations might actually develop a deeper appreciation of the self and, by extension, our clients.

Truth in fiction

Paradoxically, it is often in fiction or in the movies and on television that a more realistic portrayal of therapists is *sometimes* given, as in the television series *The Sopranos* where, during one troubling episode, the psychiatrist is sorely tempted to seek revenge on her rapist by telling her mob boss client what has happened. In Patrick McGrath's powerful novel, *Trauma* (2008), a psychiatrist is mercilessly driven by the unknown secret of his past. Fitzgerald's *Tender is the Night* (1933) tells the story of Nick Diver falling prey to the wounded charms of a patient, his narcissism leading them both towards inevitable destruction.

There are also deeply corrosive portrayals of psychiatrists and psychotherapists portrayed on the screen and in books, including Katzenbach's *The Analyst* (2002), where the eponymous hero begins as a rather stiff and repressed character and ends up akin to Rambo after being stalked by a client.

A more compassionate, but no less worrying tale is Alistair Campbell's *All in the Mind* (2008), the story of a therapist falling apart, in the end committing suicide rather than seeking help to fight his demons. Along the way he takes comfort from his clients, a questionable means of finding support and very different from deriving satisfaction through one's work. Perhaps this illustrates the dilemma of many therapists who find seeking help after qualifying more shaming than helpful, sometimes to their detriment.

The Existential therapist Irvin Yalom has written of therapeutic hubris in his novel, *Lying on the Couch* (1996), focusing on a community of therapists, some of whom are motivated by greed and the narcissistic imperative not to be seen as vulnerable. One notable character, from the beginning of the book, believes that he is above the laws and moral imperatives that underlie the basics of ethical practice. Clearly, these are therapists who risk bringing their own preoccupations into the clinical setting to the detriment of their clients. In this novel, it is the therapist who proves himself a 'good' therapist who struggles the most deeply, working hard to understand and accept his susceptibility to life's temptations.

In 2005, Paul Whitehouse brought the BBC series *Help* to the screen. Whitehouse played a series of characters, while Chris Langham portrayed the very human psychotherapist who clearly struggles in his concern and care for his patients and his helplessness at their often overwhelming need. In his personal life, he cannot even give voice to his affection for his secretary. In a terrible paradox, Langham was later embroiled in scandal, incurring a jail term for sex with an underage girl and the series ran for only one season.

The American version of the Israeli television series *In Therapy* with Gabriel Byrne is particularly evocative of the 'human' therapist who also does good work. From the first episode Byrne is face to face with the erotic transference, his own discomfort manifest in his gentle fiddling with his wedding ring. In this episode he resists, but the task is not always easy, particularly as he struggles within the apparent confines and unhappiness of his own marriage.

This is just a snapshot of the fictional literature on therapy, but it is interesting to note that it is often only in novels or in drama that we can sometimes bear to see ourselves portrayed in truly human form. The truth, perhaps, often cuts too deep a narcissistic wound. We may also fear that we will expose ourselves to personal and professional sanctions if we expose our vulnerabilities in too public a forum. Silence, then, is a form of defence, and the wider therapeutic community is deprived of the benefit of many therapists' personal experience and insight.

Therapists' distress

In my study of forty therapists, more than half of them admitted to suffering depression in the course of their professional life (Chapter 4). For some it is a 'chronic' condition, while for two-thirds of them, depression was experienced as 'episodic'.

This should come as no surprise, particularly if we take into account that therapists can usually name archaic experience as the motivating force behind their training as therapists. This also pretty much dispenses with the myth that therapists are 'untroubled', not struggling any longer with the woes of mere mortals. If we hark back to our gurus, narcissism is certainly a primary player, the perfect defence against intense feelings of inadequacy.

If we are not 'better than', we are 'less than', and being 'ordinary' is not enough to combat the terrible emptiness that a sense of inferiority brings with it. Perhaps the more tenaciously a guru clings to her high perch, the deeper runs the fear that she is actually human?

Geller, Norcross and Orlinsky (2005) directly researched therapists' distress. They studied the meaning of personal therapy in psychotherapists' lives across the modalities, including Freudian, Jungian and Cognitive Behavioural. As they point out, ' it is easier to be wise and mature for others than for ourselves'. Considering psychotherapists' struggle in personal therapy, the authors go on to point out that therapists are sometimes threatened by the notion of 'needing help', as if they will then be seen as an 'imposter' (Geller, Norcross and Orlinsky, 2005, p. 6).

So, perhaps at the deepest level we also fear that if we are not *above* our clients, we are not worthy of working with them. That 'bogeyman' again, wishing for control.

Saving ourselves

To become a therapist may be to derive satisfaction from helping others, but it is in large part also reparative, an effort to save ourselves. The psychiatrist and psychotherapist Felicity de Zulueta warns:

> It is possible that many of those who choose to train in psychotherapy have themselves suffered from deprivation and/or abuse and that they tend to deal with their own needs by projecting them and attending to them in their patients. These potential 'compulsive carers' require a personal therapeutic experience which addresses the reality of their traumatic past if they are to avoid both denying and recreating their patient's own traumatic experience within the therapeutic setting.
>
> (1993, p. 262)

In his book *A Curious Calling* (2007), Sussman also warns of ignoring our unconscious motivations for becoming therapists, of retreating behind our professional mask in order to excise our personal demons through our clients and patients. 'It is', he says, 'only when the practitioner's unconscious motivations are discovered and understood that their destructive potential can be held in check' (p. 4). I agree: we cannot afford to ignore our motivations for becoming therapists. The question we pose to our clients and patients, 'What brings you here?', must also be asked of ourselves (p. 193).

Bager-Charleson (2010) considered, with six other therapists of differing modalities within the same peer supervision group, what their motivations were for becoming therapists. As a backdrop to their reflections, Bager-

Charleson and her colleagues surveyed 238 therapists, who confirmed that their reasons for becoming therapists rested primarily in their troubled histories.

Carl Rogers, towards the end of his life, was very open about his need for intimacy, something as a younger man he often found difficult outside the therapy room. A therapist of great integrity and with an ability to establish deep relationships with his clients, he found that within the therapy room he could develop an intimacy 'without risking too much of my person' (Rogers, 1990, p. 47). Pure or impure, none the less his contribution to the welfare of his clients and countless others through his teachings has been immense.

The choice of model, too, rests in our histories, whether we are psychoanalytically bent on understanding and insight, believe in the value of congruence and unconditional positive regard, or are more inclined towards practical solutions (Chapter 6). The tradition in which we train is also a reflection of our personal philosophy, about which we perhaps think very little in our day-to-day lives, but 'act out' within the framework in which we practise psychotherapy. In our work life we are simply trying to find a way to make sense of our experience and derive meaning out of personal tragedy and archaic loss.

I believe that in this evidence of profound human frailty there is also some comfort, indicating that it may be from the position of our own vulnerability that we do our best work. However, we also have an obligation to 'model' the struggle in maintaining ethical standards, focusing on personal growth and the effort to work through our personal demons, something a number of gurus quite patently fail to do in the shame, perhaps, that they suffer the same degree of human 'imperfection' as the rest of us.

None of us are gods, and we will all return to ash and dust in the end. The very best we can offer our clients and patients is our humanity, the common denominator of human suffering and a willingness to learn from the other. As Yalom points out, it is the *relationship* that matters, and in order to have a true relationship there must be authenticity and a willingness to give (1980, p. 401). Not the details of our lives, of course, but the quality of our experience, some willingness to be used by our clients as a baby will use its mother in order to develop a sense of self. And from that we will derive our job satisfaction, some sense of achievement and meaning, as we all must in the course of our professional lives. Working as a therapist is a privilege, and with it comes a profound responsibility to know ourselves as much as we hope to know others.

2 In the family way

When therapists have children (or not)

One day a woman I had been seeing for several years began her session by announcing she was pregnant. Her blue eyes wide open, both delighted and terrified it seemed to me, she leaned forward in her seat and asked, 'Do you have children?'

I pulled up a little higher in my chair. 'I have step-children', I replied, a pusillanimous response if there ever was one.

My client sighed, closed her eyes for two or three mighty long seconds and then sat back in her seat, her shoulders a little drooped. Such disappointment!

In this chapter I explore aspects of parenthood in relation to clinical work. Is being a parent fundamental to being a good therapist? Having children can contribute towards an increase in empathy, but also sometimes act as an intrusion. Pregnancy, in either the client or the therapist, can also evoke feelings of love, hatred and envy towards the other, responses that need to be brought into awareness and 'worked through', rather than acted upon within the therapy room. Equally powerful are feelings of loss, following a miscarriage or a therapist's simple longing for parenthood. And what of the children themselves: what does it mean to be the offspring of therapists, many of whose parents are often preoccupied with their clients, or who cannot leave their professional lives behind at the office?

The childless therapist

But back to my response to my client, who asked the question, 'Do you have children?' You may be a therapist who believes in revealing something personal, in which case my stating the literal truth isn't an issue. But the fact that I became defensive in the face of a perfectly ordinary and urgent question on the part of my patient *is* important. This was a case in point where my personal life directly affected the way I responded to a client.

Maroda rightly argues from a psychoanalytic perspective that there are moments when revealing something of ourselves can be deeply meaningful and 'illuminating' for the client (2004, p. 4). But she also points out that defensiveness is *always* significant, indicating 'a counter-transference problem, no matter how small or transient. Whenever a therapist removes himself from the patient for any reason the countertransference is dominating and obstructing the treatment' (p. 123).

Kahn, in his seminal text, *Between Therapist and Client,* agrees, 'When we are threatened in any way, the temptation to fight back, to explain, to justify, to one-up, to go coldly silent is almost overwhelming in all but saints, and there are few saints in our profession' (2000, p. 16). A non-defensive approach, he argues, is fundamental to the development of a healthy working alliance.

My client wanted reassurance and there are any number of ways I might have responded more appropriately. I had worked with her for several years and so might have asked her *why* she was asking the question, and thereby learned more about her anxieties. I could have inquired about what it might mean for her if I did, or didn't have children. Aware of her concern, I could have reflected it back to her: 'You're worried perhaps, that I won't understand if I have never had children?' I more or less got around to these points eventually, and ultimately I think she even began to trust me on the matter, or at least she began to trust herself more and keep faith with her own experience.

I, on the other hand, have puzzled over my defensiveness since, recognising that often when it comes to the crunch with a patient who is pregnant, I feel inadequate as a therapist.

Longing for motherhood

There is a widespread assumption these days that if you really want children you can have them. IVF, fertility drugs, surrogates, and insemination have all made the likelihood of giving birth much more possible for those who just a generation ago would not have been able to become parents. However, there are many people for whom these medical interventions are not possible, for either medical or personal reasons. Sometimes it is a matter of conscience.

In my study, five therapists mentioned not having children, all of them women. For three of them this was cited as a personal sorrow, while another spoke of her choice not to have children as a way of putting a stop to the violence and mental instability that ran like a thread through several generations of her family's history. But Alice focused on her longing for a family as the central point of her personal life, around which the whole of her professional life was built.

Case study: childlessness

Alice is a therapist on the verge of retirement, slowly closing down her practice in the north of England as each of her patients leaves. She has worked as a psychoanalytic therapist for over thirty years, coming into the profession after working as a physician with a voluntary organisation in Africa. While there, and working particularly with mothers and children, she discovered that she was fascinated by the 'emotional side' of medicine. When she returned to the UK after a decade away she found settling into the demands and structure of the NHS very difficult. 'Training as a psychotherapist just seemed the next logical step,' she said. By any standards her career as a psychotherapist has been successful: for many years she headed a large, voluntary counselling centre in a deprived area of Newcastle, while also working in private practice. She is also an established author, having written a seminal text focusing particularly on bereavement.

I met Alice in her home where she lives alone and still runs her practice. The living room was small but comfortable and the mantelpiece was covered with framed photographs of smiling children. She was gracious and dignified and throughout the interview sat with a labrador to the side of her chair, gently stroking its ears. After telling me a little about her history and her time in Africa, she spoke about the deep pain at the centre of her personal life, the one, she says, she has never been able to reconcile:

> If I regret anything in life [it's] that I didn't have children, and I know that's influenced me with clients [and] patients, and I do have quite a strong maternal instinct, and people pick it up. Whether I would have been different if I'd had children, I don't know.

Alice worked with many children in Africa 'who were needing to be looked after' and she admitted that she had sometimes considered adopting one of them. However, her status as a single woman finally prevented her and she returned to England on her own. She admits there were links between her choice of professions and her longing for children. Patients and trainee therapists both helped to mitigate her sense of loss, though never to extinguish the grief altogether. Sometimes she had to manage difficult bouts of envy and, at other times, shame that she was not in an intimate relationship and had no children:

> I've always been single ... I think it's difficult not to feel that there's some sort of deficit in your life really, and I was aware. I've always been aware and worried about it actually, worried about whether you are somehow using your clients, you know, to fulfil that sort of intimacy because it is a very intimate [relationship] ...

Still quietly stroking her dog, she articulated the familiar conflict between knowing and wishing that who we are, and what we feel, will not impact negatively on our work:

> I wouldn't like to pretend that they've [patients] never met any need of mine, because I know they will have done. And I know that some of them probably did without me knowing it ... I've done a lot of training, training of doctors originally and then of student counsellors or psychotherapists. I think that that's been some sublimation of [my longing for children] because you've got the younger generation and you're preparing them for the world, you know, so I think ... and I feel that's okay, really, because I think why not? If you don't have your own children, why not use your abilities to help other people, after all there's enough people in the world that need it, you know, so I think ... I don't feel too bad about that at all.

Alice also expressed the difficulty of coming to terms with such a personal grief, an ongoing sorrow that never really settled down completely and needed re-visiting in therapy at various stages of her life. It was certainly not something to be 'sorted' during her training analysis, never to be discussed again:

> it's a continuing situation. It's not ever something you ever get over, in my experience anyway. Well I say you get over it, you get over it, but I mean each stage in life you have to, like any sort of grief, you have to re-work it again.

Even now, as she moves into retirement, she feels most acutely the loss of the children she never had:

> From my point of view, my own viewpoint of it is that it's such a painful area for me, and interestingly enough, this year, I've been quite ill. I have some very good friends and people looked after me, but I was very aware then of not having adult children who would have rallied round, you know, so that's what I meant by every stage in life you have to re-play it.

Sitting in the room with Alice, her pain was palpable. For Alice, the absence of children is a subject for re-negotiation at every stage of her life, and is, of itself, *the* significant event in her life, unconsciously guiding her towards her choice of professions, first of all as a physician, and later as a therapist and teacher. She has returned to therapy on a variety of occasions to work through, yet again, her grief over not having children. At each stage of her life she has missed them in a different way. It is the pain she has carried with her most acutely into her work with clients, enabling her to tune in more empathically most of the time and, in other moments, it has evoked powerful feelings of envy or shame in her that she, too, is not a mother. But most importantly, she has tried to make sense of her experience, and be aware as much as possible of the role it has played in her professional life with clients and trainees.

Facing the void

There was a time within my busy practice when it seemed to me that nearly every woman I saw under the age of forty became pregnant. This isn't unusual of course. These are childbearing years and often what brings people to therapy are struggles with forming meaningful relationships and fear that their chance of creating a family is passing.

The assumption on the part of most of my patients is that I have children, that I have given birth, raised and nurtured my offspring successfully into adulthood. As a result, I will understand and empathise with their fears, their struggles with love and hate towards their offspring and the effort of keeping an adult relationship alive in the face of parental demands. How I have managed this, happily or otherwise, will depend on their own experience with 'mother'.

Clients have also, at times, assumed that I have been abused, anorexic or traumatised, otherwise how could I 'know' so well what they are suffering. Beyond my defensiveness regarding motherhood, and never having experienced the agony of a miscarriage or the death of child directly, I have had to *imagine* the loss, sometimes of course absorbing my patient's projections when their grief is simply too great for them to bear on their own.

Therapy, I believe, is a creative process.[1] Like any other artistic endeavour it demands imagination, the ability to transcend what *is*, and to imagine what *could be*. It is on the basis of this that I am able to empathise with my patients' experiences, which are often very removed from, or variant with, my own. It is the same unconscious process at work that enables me to write works of fiction, with characters who conduct themselves differently than I do, and whose presentation in the world is not mine. There is a morsel of me in them somewhere, of course, but essentially it is my unconscious creativity which allows me to empathise with those imaginary characters and create a life for them. As I do with my patients. My empathy comes from other challenges in life, not from the echo of common experience, and certainly not in the case of parenthood.

Firsthand experience

The general consensus among therapists in my study was that any common experience contributes to their ability to empathise with others. This was particularly true around parenthood. Therapists of all persuasions, both men and women, spoke of having children as deepening their ability to make contact:

> I think it gives me more insight into a lot of the work I do ... With a lot of people who present ... some of their difficulties are when they've just had children, obviously, because it triggers off their early infantile experiences or family experiences, so you know it [having my own children] sort of helped ... helped me understand. Like, if a patient's got twins and exhausted or excited about something, I feel I can empathise with a lot of the experiences, real experiences, you know, not theoretical.

Working with students at the start of their training, and before they begin their clinical practice, it is obvious that they are considering things from a theoretical standpoint, without any benefit of the lived experience within the therapy room. This is the difference between our knowing something theoretically and *really* knowing it. I liken this to medical students working on a cadaver to practise their surgery skills; this is surely very different from leaning over to cut into a live, pulsating body. And a mock trial for a trainee lawyer can't possibly replicate the tensions of a real court room. So, despite my earlier argument, and according to many therapists, *imagining* giving birth or parenthood is not quite enough, perhaps. As Terry reinforces, there's nothing quite like firsthand experience:

> Before you're a parent yourself, you can read all the books in the world, you can talk to all the parents in the world, but you don't have that personal experience to draw from. I had a quite difficult birth with my daughter, very difficult birth, very traumatic birth, and when I hear traumatic births from parents, that really sits with me.

Having children increases insight and empathy for the complexities of family life, but as Guy (1987) argues, for therapists there may be an additional significance: 'Parenthood is an important developmental stage encountered by most psychotherapists. Its profound impact on the personal life of the therapist cannot help but have an effect on his or her practice of psychotherapy at one time or another' (p. 161).

John, another CBT therapist, agrees. Having children has given him a deeper understanding of the more subtle aspects of clinical work, enabling him to conceptualise therapy as a 'development in process'. He also believes that in forming positive relationships with his children, he has come to understand, fundamentally, the importance of establishing a 'working alliance' with his clients:

> My children are now 16 and 12 and so they're great kids, but like any kids, we've gone through some rough patches ... The thing that's always been [at] the forefront of how I want to parent is really maintaining a good relationship with my kids, and so whether the issue is, you know, she lied to me about this or that, or didn't live up to her responsibility, or what have you, that broader sense of, okay whatever happens here in terms of sorting this out, I want to come through the other end with a good relationship with her, and I guess ... I'm trying to connect the dots here, so that's the sort of sense of ... in the same way I have with my clients. I want to maintain a good therapeutic relationship, and part of that is, I guess, conceptualising them at some level as going through some developmental work. (John, CBT)

In both Terry's and John's cases, having children has opened them up to a greater understanding of child development processes, aspects of theory which may not have been so heavily focused on within their training. However, therapists in *every* tradition pointed out that giving birth, or being a parent, contributed to a greater empathy towards their clients and patients, and a deeper understanding of the complex issues surrounding parenthood.

Parenthood: a divided loyalty?

But what of the dangers? Like any working mother, a therapist parent may also struggle with leaving her child behind with a nanny or childminder, or their first days in school.

Claire Basescu's father was a psychologist–psychoanalyst, practising from an office in their family home. Forever intrigued by what went on behind those closed doors, she now writes from the perspective of a working psychotherapist–parent herself (2001). She points out that parenthood, a source of 'creative tension in the therapist' (p. 103), can also tip into guilt. Returning to work after the birth of a child she experienced 'acute separation anxiety and wondered if my children did also' (p. 111). She also considered whether she was 'short changing' her patients:

> when patients talk about their childhoods and the impact of their parents, I sometimes find myself thinking, oh, I have to remember never to do that or that's something to try to do. I find myself thinking about my children at a case conference or in a session when an event

is being discussed that occurred at an age that is close to that of one of my children. This can be helpful because it gives me a developmental context with which to evaluate the event being described. It can also be distracting, excruciating, and anxiety provoking as I think about my own child's vulnerability. (p. 114)

So nothing is straightforward – what is helpful can also be distracting. What we learn from our children at home, we can apply in our work, and the reverse is also true, allowing us to bring greater understanding to our role as parents.

The struggle to stay awake ...

How often have I heard clients speak of a former therapist who 'fell asleep' during a session? Aware that I have struggled at times to keep my eyes open, often due to counter-transferential elements within the therapy, but sometimes due to tiredness after a sleepless night, or the exhausting elements of personal crisis, I am only lucky that I haven't dozed off entirely! Now I wonder if any of these therapists who did clock off completely, for at least a few minutes, were parents.

Patrick, a humanistic therapist, runs a university counselling department and is the father of three children, all under the age of five. Having a family, he says, is a mixed blessing when it comes to his work with patients. While it has increased his sensitivity to the distress of many of the kids he sees in his work within the Australian school system, the sleep deprivation he suffers as a result of interrupted nights also plays havoc with his ability to remember detail, as he explained with some humour:

Negatively, it probably affects certainly my memory. I can't pretend that I'm going to remember if a client did ask me, yesterday or the day before, where were we last week ... I can't pretend that I'm going to remember everything ... I notice that I just accept culpability for everything now. If somebody says I sent you this or I did that, I'm just thinking, yeah I know you must have done and I've just forgotten about it because repeatedly I have the experience of not even remembering a conversation, let alone [anything else]!

Patrick may be referring to the exhausting work of being a parent, but he may also be speaking for anyone who is worn out, caring for an ill relative perhaps, or facing a personal challenge that is preventing them from getting enough sleep. Patrick claimed, however, that this very vulnerability may also carry a constructive element:

Ironically there is a sort of positive in that too ... something about acceptance. There is something about me being tender with my own limitations that allows me, and sensitises me, to the things other people face and other people's limitations, and helps, maybe, through my acceptance of that for them to be more tolerant of their own.

For Patrick, then, there is also a positive in his current emotional predicament. As a father of young children he is vulnerable to exhaustion and lapses of memory. He is apparently non-defensive in his approach with his clients, unafraid to expose his fragility at the moment to his clients, not so much by what he says, but by *how* he is with clients. If he can be 'tender' towards himself during this demanding period of fatherhood, so may his clients learn to be tender towards themselves as well.

Children as interruptions and intrusions

Michelle works within a busy, demanding community health clinic. While she and her partner longed for children, the result was not quite what they had expected. After several years of IVF treatment, in itself often experienced as stressful and invasive, she gave birth to twins:

> there was sort of frustration because I was struggling with starting a family and then for about eight years I had a couple of early miscarriages. But then we did – we were successful with IVF and we had twins, which is not as it was meant to be, and then the whole pregnancy was a risk, [there were] complications ... but we were blessed. And then, on a bad day, on a negative day, you think I'm quite burdened by two, two healthy children at once, they're now 14, so ...

While becoming a parent may increase a therapist's capacity to empathise with his or her patients, there can certainly be drawbacks, elements that can cause a rupture to the working alliance or cause the therapist to be preoccupied with more immediate concerns. Terry spoke earlier of her increased empathy towards her clients as a result of becoming a mother, but parenthood has also, at times, interfered with her work. Both her young children suffer with severe allergies:

> I think I have to be very careful that I stay with the client in the room, and that my mind doesn't go to my children. I think that generally works fine, but I had a particularly difficult experience when I was seeing a parent of a child actually, and what happened was someone phoned the clinic while I was in session and the secretary knocked on the door and

said 'I'm sorry but the nurse has phoned and it's an emergency'. And so I had to come and deal with that and that was really hard because the client was feeling like she shouldn't be there because, you know, she knew that I was having problems with my children, and I felt I needed to finish the session. So I finished the session with her, but I found it very difficult and I found it very hard to kind of keep a path with her really, and I think she probably picked that up, and we finished quite rapidly.

This raises a question, of course, concerning first of all our ability to remain psychologically connected with our patients at times of stress, and secondly how we manage what could happen unexpectedly. With two young allergy-prone children it could be argued that having a session interrupted might be a predictable scenario. On the other hand, how much, or how likely is it to interfere with this patient at this particular time? How much do we self-disclose, or build in to the relationship the possibility of what *might* happen, and probably won't, but *will* happen with someone at some point? As Norcross and Guy (2007) point out:

> Parenthood supplies an assortment of disruption in the therapist's relationships with clients. Children become ill, break limbs, and need their parents in emergencies. These realities of parenting increase the complexity of our professional role and necessitate a precarious balancing act to meet the fluid needs of both children and parents. (p. 54)

Basescu (2001) also writes of being so disturbed at news of her child that a patient recognised she was not equipped to work and so walked out of the session. This later provided rich, analytic material, but it is also indicative of the pressures facing a therapist who is working hard to fulfil her duties both on a personal and a professional front. My guess is that there is no way around this tension completely and may, in fact, echo the same anxieties within many of our clients who struggle between the demands of their professional lives and those of their families.

Children as a reason to live

In my experience, suicidal clients often cite children as the single most important factor preventing them from taking action. Therapists are no less vulnerable to the stresses and strains of life and may be even more vulnerable because of their exposure to life's more disturbing elements through their work with clients. While I write of depression in therapists in Chapter 4, I think it is worth noting here that children may also keep therapists alive, as in the case of Edith.

Case study: staying alive

Edith is a humanistic practitioner of many years' standing, having trained a large number of the therapists now working in Brisbane, Australia. Held in great respect by her pupils and colleagues, they might be very surprised to hear how vulnerable she once felt. During our interview in her office, she spoke of a very 'low' period in her life when her marriage was disintegrating, 'but I didn't know it yet'.

Edith was attending a 'continuing professional development' workshop when she was struck by the realisation that she was 'preparing to die'. This came as a profound shock to her, realising that she was saying to herself, 'I need to stay alive until my daughter is launched, when I am 59'. A colleague/ therapist did not laugh when she said this to him in a practice session, but rather reflected back to her the serious sentiment behind the statement. Paradoxically, this revelation of her inner struggle and unconscious workings came as a huge relief to Edith and, when she returned to work, a client commented that she seemed to be so much more 'present' than previously. Therapy with this client, she said, progressed 'more quickly' after that. It was through this experience that she realised how preoccupied she had been up until then with her unacknowledged distress, which had also been 'leaking' into her work. Edith's marriage of 23 years ended soon after, the conscious acceptance of her distress finally prompting her to take action in her personal life too.

This paradox of what is known but not consciously acknowledged between therapist and client, as in Edith's case, echoes Bollas's 'unthought known' (1987). As in Chapter 5, where therapists illustrate their *wish* that their personal anxieties might be kept out of the therapy room, in fact this may be impossible. As Edith discovered, whatever both the patient and the therapist bring of themselves into the therapy room, regardless of whether it is consciously acknowledged or not, undoubtedly impacts the work and the relationship.

The pregnant therapist

A pregnant therapist introduces a third party into the relationship.

I find it interesting that in my study not a single female therapist mentioned the impact of her pregnancy on her work. In my experience with pregnant clients, there is often a tendency not to venture too deeply into their material for fear of 'harming' their baby. Already they are protecting the child they carry within.

Would this not also be true for therapists working during their pregnancy, often until quite close to their due date? Pregnancy in the therapist can evoke powerful feelings in a patient, replicating earlier experiences of abandonment and neglect and sibling rivalry writ large in the therapy room. There may be unconscious fantasies of 'killing' the foetus, of doing away with what stands between the patient and the 'therapeutic mother'. How does a therapist protect herself and her baby, and the client too as she moves from the therapy room into giving birth and attending to her child over and above her patients?

Like Basescu (2001) earlier, a pregnant therapist must struggle between the demands of her work life, and the responsibilities and yearnings of impending motherhood. Etchegoyen (1993) became pregnant 'late in life'. She articulates some of the difficulties she faced in working throughout her pregnancy:

> I had to keep an open mind about the way I was being perceived in the transference and about my countertransference responses. It required consistent and at times painful working through on my part, e.g. it was an unexpected discovery for me to realise that I was envious of the youth of my child patient and his parents. It was hard work to disentangle my guilt about having a baby, my fears of 'evil attacks' towards the foetus and my mourning over my decision to give up work prematurely.

She also writes of her powerful feelings of competition towards colleagues who were making efforts to help with clients she had to 'abandon' to look after her own child.

Cullington-Roberts argues that when pregnancy does harm the work, it must be acknowledged: 'Patients and therapist alike may deny that any damage has occurred or, if it has, defensively reassure themselves that they are blameless. Rather than offer containment and possible insight, the risk is of therapy itself becoming a re-enactment of trauma' (2004, p. 100).

It is in the acknowledgement of that possible 're-enactment' that the potential for insight and reparation exists. If we are the products of our own stories, we can also reconfigure them, make sense of ourselves both as therapists and as clients, in a deeper understanding of own narrative. Through discussion and acceptance of what we find most difficult, both within and without, we can at least have hope.

Work vs family concerns

Parenthood highlights the tension and effort many therapists face in *giving* to their families in the same way that they *give* at the office. We are not bottomless in our ability to listen and empathise, and we may want a bit of it ourselves when we're home, not the other way around. Norcross and Guy

(2007) claim that 75 per cent of therapists complain that their work life spills over into their home life. 'The therapist's family may come to resent the energy and caring that seems more available to patients. Exhorting clients to devote more time and energy to nurturing their own family may take on an empty, even hypocritical, ring to many therapists neglecting their own' (p. 54). This in turn can lead to marital difficulties, often culminating in divorce (Chapter 7). Wheels within wheels, this can 'precipitate therapists' anxiety over its possible discovery by patients or cause doubts concerning competency since their marriage has failed' (Guy, 1987; Norcross and Guy, 2007, p. 55).

Being a therapist is very hard work. Ours is not a straightforward job, with specific tasks that enable us to 'zone out' at times, and think of other things. Our job is to focus on the hard-core experiences of the other, and when we do find ourselves wondering, or fantasising, we have an obligation to determine what it might mean. We are forever on task while at the office and sitting across from our patient. And even when we are not, we sometimes need to reflect on what has just happened, we may need to gain some perspective, to consider the degree of disturbance in our client, or in ourselves, or both. Sometimes this can mean there is not much left over for the emotional requirements that being a parent, a partner, or a good friend actually requires.

We are bound by confidentiality, so there's no talking about what we do when we come home. This can be particularly stressful in small communities, where everyone tends to be connected to everyone else.[2] Of necessity, we work alone, which can provide us with the kind of intimacy we long for (Rogers, 1990, p. 47), but may isolate us further in the long run if we do not ensure that we maintain strong links within the therapeutic community. These are relationships that can sustain and support us through difficult times, often helping us to put our work in context. Without a life outside the office, we are vulnerable to boundary violations, including those of a sexual nature.[3] Isolated from others, both physically and intellectually, we can begin to rationalise anything, to justify anything. Balancing our family life, then, becomes essential in maintaining rhythm and order in our lives and often provides the meaning we need *outside* the therapy room.

Becoming a parent does not automatically turn us into good people. As my colleague, David Mann, points out, motherhood is certainly transformational, but not always for the good. What might promote a deeper capacity for empathy, may also evoke sadistic tendencies. 'There are too many cruel mothers and neglected children in the world to believe in the maternal instinct,' he says, warning us of the seductive nature of idealisation (personal communication). While we focus on the positive, there is always the shadow to be considered. Melanie Klein was never noted for her own mothering skills, and, as noted in Chapter 1, Ronald Laing's son claimed his relationship with his father 'improved' substantially following his death (Laing, 2006).

The kids are all right?

My father was an obstetrician and gynaecologist. The schoolyard joke was that my father liked women. I didn't find this tired old line so much funny as I did predictable and sometimes irritating. Therapists' and psychiatrists' kids also had to bear the brunt of jokes, the assumption that they were a little nuts *because* they were children of 'shrinks', as we called them. All psychiatrists were crazy, of course they were. I have no idea now why, or how, we came to hold these notions, but they seemed to be in the zeitgeist, permeating even the frozen north where I lived in a mid-sized Canadian city in the middle of the prairie.

My own step-children are in a bit of trouble on that score. Their father is an educational psychologist and both their mother and step-mother are psychotherapists, one wag pointing out that my husband simply decided to change therapists. Another perspective might be that neither of us were therapists when we first married him, but were ultimately driven into the profession.

I decided to go to the source, and ask my step-daughter directly how it was for her. 'It made me really well balanced,' she quipped. 'My brother and I called the patients the "loons". Here comes a "loon", we used to say,' perhaps by this means establishing a firm distinction between themselves and those strangers coming into the home.

Though she was a teenager by the time her mother began training, eventually patients were seen at home. 'It was mildly inconvenient', she says. The benefit of her mother's choice of profession, and what she appreciates deeply these days, is her therapist–parent's ability to ask the appropriate question, cutting straight to an issue. 'What was irritating to live with back then is now a real help.' These days a working mother of twins, she sees both her parents as 'resources', reassuring and normalising her children's stages of growth. 'It's a lot easier to appreciate what they do when you're not living with them!' she says, reaping the benefit of 'insider' knowledge on child development and the human psyche. 'Even friends ask me what my father would think about something, and they like talking to my mom about stuff.'

Walking on eggshells

A number of years ago, a colleague asked if she could rent my office for an afternoon a week while she was winding down her practice after moving out of the area. This seemed an agreeable arrangement, my office being at the very back of the house, arrived at directly along a hallway away from the house 'proper'. For the first time I became aware of what it must be like for others at home while I was working. Self-conscious and restricted, it limited my actions (no running down the hallway, or pounding up the stairs!), and how much noise I could make (no raised voices, or shouting for joy!), and listening to Emmylou Harris on the down low. It wasn't exactly a tip-toe existence, but hardly represented freedom of movement either. Quite simply, I didn't like it. For family members it can be hard going when they are forced to stay out of certain rooms during particular times of the day. One friend of mine, the partner of a therapist with an office in the basement, tells me he wants to scream sometimes when he is forced to stay out of the dining room, situated directly above the office. Another friend has spoken of being obliged to keep her young children at the front of their flat when her partner is working at the back, and to keep them silent – no mean feat when they are both under five years of age.

In a small-scale study of therapists' children in New York City, Golden and Farber (1998) discovered that these kids were generally comfortable with their parents' profession, though they didn't enjoy the intrusion into their lives with late night phone calls and sometimes having to be quiet while their therapist–parent attended to clients. Between the ages of 10 and 18, many of these children also expressed appreciation for their therapist–parent's sensitivity and skill in managing crises, and their tolerance for subjects others might consider uncomfortable. What the kids did resent was a parent acting like a therapist at home, becoming too intrusive or a 'know-it-all'. As the authors point out, 'Children of therapists do not wish to be treated as being in constant need of help. What may be perceived by patients as a well-meaning and sensitive statement may be perceived by children as intrusive or patronizing' (p. 139).

This cautionary statement is made far more forcefully by Maeder, himself the child of a therapist. 'It is harder to be a good parent than it is a good therapist' (1990, p. 8), he says, pointing out that whatever benefits a child receives from a therapist–parent are the results of 'personality and affection, not the consequence of theoretical training'.

The children in both studies often 'role-played', one 12-year-old boy indicating his pleasure at pretending to be a therapist. 'I would just say "uh-huh" five hundred times' (Golden and Farber, 1998, p. 136). Another child spoke of her parent's tendency to continually check her emotional temperature, 'And how does that make you feeeeeeel?' she mocked (p. 137). According to Cray and Cray (1977), when asked what he wanted to be when he grew up, the child of one therapist responded, 'A patient' (p. 338).

Parenthood: a balancing act

The challenge for therapists is to maintain a balance. If a therapist's home life is difficult, there will be consequences at the office, perhaps an over-reliance on the client to bring satisfaction, to bolster up a 'self' that may feel wounded or inadequate elsewhere. Deriving job satisfaction is one thing, but in our profession there is a responsibility not to rely on our clients for personal gratification, particularly at the expense of their emotional development.

Raskin, a former student and colleague of Carl Rogers, articulated his personal struggle to be a better man at home, or at least as good a man as he was at the office:

> Not that the struggle to be more personal, human and authentic as a therapist or as a client is easy. But I have found it easi-**er**. Easier to be more intimate and loving. Thus, I feel that I have thrived in the office and in weekend retreat, as have many of my clients and colleagues.
>
> (Raskin, 1978, p. 364)

He admits he finds it difficult to express his 'deep love' for his children. From his wife and his family he 'expects' that he will be 'taken care' of without 'being explicit'. And finally, he admits, he wants 'to be loved intimately, without being intimate myself' (p. 365). It is, it turns out, easier for him to *give* at the office.

It can be difficult to shed the comforting cloak of professional perspective at the door of the therapy room and re-enter family life. We are far less likely to be idealised at home. Our partners might want us to take out the rubbish, the kids might be cranky and lord knows you're exhausted after seeing patients all day. If life is tough at home, there may be an additional impetus to be valued at the office. How easy is it then, to allow our patients to express anger, or disappointment, and to rage against our inability to give them *everything*. In an effort to bolster ourselves we may cross boundaries, make interventions that are inappropriate but ensure we feel better, and delude ourselves that we are doing a splendid job with this or that client. Who else could work with them as well as we do?

My own preference for re-entry into family life when I work from home is an hour of junk television, preferably with humour. The canned laughter drives my husband nuts, but I am a more cheerful as a result when I lift myself off the couch and join him for dinner. Working in an office an hour's drive away several days a week, music is fundamental. I can sing to every sad song along the route, or pound it out to Bruce Springsteen.

Our families may expect us to make the transition eagerly and easily, but movement from the troubled inner world of our patients to the external world of family and friends is not so simple. If we are truly engaged with our clients, we need some *space* in which we can move from one state of mind to the other. This can be even more difficult when we work from home, and there is no 'commute' during which to shed the tensions of our day. We may also need to remind ourselves that in the push and pull of our relationships, to be human is not a failing but a strength, and none of us is omnipotent.

Growing up?

Returning to the issue of 'childlessness', what does it mean for a therapist who is longing for children to be facing a patient who is pregnant, or considering abortion? What unconscious feelings of envy, or resentment, what elements of unacknowledged hate might be stirring beneath the surface of compassionate understanding?

This most fundamental of human experiences may also be the source of the most primal of emotions within a counselling setting.

Earlier I referred to Guy (1987), who suggested that parenthood was important in the development of 'most therapists' (p. 161). What then, does it mean for those therapists who do not have children? Certainly this may account for some of my own defensiveness, as if I have missed out somehow, and am not quite so 'legitimate' as those of my colleagues who are parents. This may even be the professional equivalent of a mother of a young woman asking when on earth her daughter is going to provide her with grandchildren, as if this is the 'correct' way to proceed in life.

Are we, those therapists without children of our own, actually not so 'grown up' as those therapists who do? Some of us are 'barren' in the old-fashioned way, unable to have children, while others of us have elected to be childless. We, perhaps, have had to reach adulthood through other accommodations, including isolation from our peers, loneliness, the obligation to derive meaning and purpose elsewhere and, as Alice illustrated, sometimes thorough a profound sense of loss for what is longed for and cannot be had.

My defensiveness with my client surely informs me that somewhere within myself I believe that I am not bringing to my work as a therapist something that other 'adult' therapists who have children certainly do. Am I the therapeutic equivalent of the daughter who has not produced grandchildren?

Neither Donald Winnicott nor Anna Freud, two therapists who profoundly influenced how we view children today, were parents. That Winnicott had a mischievous (childish?) streak can't be denied – for instance driving his open-topped car standing up with his head through the roof and his walking stick on the pedal, or riding his bicycle downhill with his feet on the handlebars – but the beauty of his writing and the importance of his observations are also a powerful testimony to his intellectual maturity (Jacobs, 1995).

Despite birth control, and new perspectives on unconventional lifestyles, Bonnici (2011) refers to the insistence of several of her therapists over the years to consider her choice not to be a mother as a form of abnormality. This may reflect a general view on the part of some therapists that not having children is an aberration; in the same way that homosexuality was once considered an unacceptable deviation from the 'norm'. To suffer with longing for children is one thing, choosing not to have them quite another.

This, however, was not my experience, even as a young woman in my twenties. A therapist posing the question, 'why not have children?' in my case did not necessarily imply judgement so much as an opportunity to think through the issue. To defend a decision is different from defensiveness, hunkering down or attacking. Through the uncomfortable process of deliberation, I may maintain, or change my decision, but in the end it will rest on a more solid foundation than current rationalisation of an unconscious, archaic, defence.

Conclusion

Parenthood is a fundamental human experience, valued by therapists who have a family as essential in their development as therapists. Having children deepens their empathy, but also establishes a greater tension between their professional and family lives. No therapist, I suggest, wants their child to be so full of longing that they dream of one day being their therapist–parent's 'patient'.

And for the therapist without a family, there may be longing, envy and unconscious hatred towards those for whom pregnancy appears to come easily. For some therapists, like myself, there may be feelings of inadequacy facing clients who are pregnant. My compassion for their ambivalence and fear must come from other challenges in my life, not common experience. In that very lack of experience, I am forced to grow up and contain my client as best I can, just as a mother would, and be a 'good enough' therapist.

Notes

1 Akeret, R. U. (1995), *The Man Who Loved a Polar Bear*. London: Penguin Books; Bugental, J. F. T. (1992), *The Art of Psychotherapy*. New York: W.W. Norton; Storr, A. (1990), *The Art of Psychotherapy*. (second edn). Oxford: Butterworth-Heinemann.

2 Beskind, H., Bartels, S. J. and Brooks, M. (1993), 'Practical and Theoretical Dilemmas of Dynamic Psychotherapy in a Small Community'. In J. H. Gold

and J. C. Nemiah (eds), *Beyond Transference*. Washington, DC: American Psychiatric Press.
3 Kottler, J. A. (2010), *On Being a Therapist*. San Francisco, CA: Jossey-Bass; Mann, D. (1997), *Psychotherapy: An Erotic Relationship, Transference and Countertransference Passions*. London: Routledge; Rutter, P. (1989), *Sex in the Forbidden Zone*. New York: Fawcett Columbine.

3   Body and soul

Working while in physical pain

When I was nineteen I had an operation on both my legs. The night before, two doctors stood at the end of my bed and suggested that I might like to have the legs done six months apart, rather than have both operated on the next day. My adolescent logic in full swing, I opted for the original plan, believing a double whammy would make me special. It was a good decision. The pain was so great, it did not matter whether it was one leg or two and I'm not sure I could have faced the prospect of undergoing the same thing again six months later. I knew then, and I know now, that I spared myself something awful.

Since then I have also gone to great lengths to avoid subsequent operations. Many years later I still exercise regularly to strengthen the muscles around my knees. But I play hard too, skiing regularly and trail running, almost defying the notion that my legs are anything but normal. Staving off another operation and keeping that pain at bay has been a primary motivator for much of my life.

But paradoxically I cannot conjure up that pain now, I can only remember what I felt and thought *about* it. I remember my relationship with it, but not the pain itself. I remember the despair, the relentlessness ferocity of the experience, the breathtaking moments when the slightest twinge set the ragged edges of my poor bones scraping against one another, igniting red hot flashes of such intensity that I nearly passed out. I remember lying in bed, straight as an arrow because I could not move or bend, the whole of my lower body a dark pulsating space. I remember the grief, and the dawning realisation that this was my lot, my turn.

This chapter highlights the impact and effectiveness of therapists when they are themselves experiencing pain or illness and what this might mean within the therapeutic relationship. Once again, what might deepen the possibilities for empathy with our patients may also interfere with our ability to concentrate and focus at times. Pain has the capacity, when very intense, to blot out the world, and the anxiety that it might return lingers like the longest night.

Pain: a universal experience

Pain is pedestrian. It affects everyone. There is no one in the world who has not suffered pain. Money can't spare you, nor can intellect or fame. Pain can't be reasoned away, or ignored. By its very nature it will follow you down into every hole in which you try to seek shelter, or every activity with which you choose to distract yourself. Medicine may mask the pain and drive it underground for a while, but it is still there, ready to break through when the drug wears off or the distraction grows thin.

My defence against the pain at that early stage was to read, immersing myself in the agony of Somerset Maugham's complete short stories and, to my mother's horror, in Kubler-Ross (1969), whose book *On Death and Dying* had just been published. Remember, I was only nineteen, though unconsciously I must have understood something about the nature of illness and coming to terms with loss. I would never again take the health of my legs for granted. My running and skiing, I know, are my defences against 'death' and the passing of youth. I am driven, if you like, to prove to myself that I am not dead yet, not even lame, as all of those doctors suggested I would be this many years down the line.

Pain is also, perhaps, topographical, on the surface of life. While there, it cannot be denied. Think of a toothache, or a tension headache. A migraine will fell even the toughest soul, laying them helplessly low, sometimes for days. Backache, tennis elbow, an ingrown toenail, Lord, how these can interfere with life, distracting us from pleasure and every good intention. More deeply held, however, is our fear of death, a sense of mortality that each of these occasions brings to the fore. Our bodies change and wither, no matter how drastic the measures we take and, even when life passes slowly, death creeps closer.

There is a distinction, of course, between illness and pain. We can be very ill without experiencing that 'surface' pain, as in the early stages of cancer. But each has its legacy. Only through a dilution or repression of the memory of pain in childbirth can a woman face the prospect again. We may forget that tension headache, or at least we will lose the conscious memory, but with intense pain there is also trauma. The insidious legacy of a serious illness is a sense of loss and a fear of death, the undeniable awareness that we are mortal, and that it can happen again.

Case study: living with pain

> With the pain in my joints, I didn't think I had to stop working, because it's a chronic condition. With the cancer I wasn't sure and when I first saw the surgeon, when she heard that I was a therapist, the first thing she said is, 'you must stop working', and I thought, ohh, wooow, so I

was sort of concerned about that. I think … I can never rule out that it's a possibility. I do think that we're all sort of wounded and in pain, all of us, as therapists, as clients, so I suppose I would consider it if it was interfering dramatically with my work.

Carmen, a humanistic practitioner, recently had to deal with breast cancer and the ensuing operation to remove a lump. But more than this, since childhood she has suffered with a chronic bone condition, a debilitating and painful illness which periodically flares up, increasingly so over the past few years. While she is in remission at the moment, the intense pain of her disease when it is active is something she has had to manage intermittently for years, even as she has continued working:

> When I have been in pain, I have tried for it not to impact on our sessions and the way I've done that is by holding in my awareness my own pain. Sometimes it's just a sort of awareness of a pain on the back burner, so to speak, and other times it's more of a struggle.

Despite medication and her best efforts to manage her pain, Carmen found that it did sometimes interfere with her work:

> I would feel that I wasn't as present for my client as I would wish for, not that I didn't hear them at all … But just that my level of presence was not as … I wasn't at my best, so I would feel that there was something distracting me from my availability to the client. I suppose, coming back to person-centred principles, it would impact them in perhaps not being fully received. Perhaps that might be their experience, or perhaps not feeling completely confident in the sense of unconditional positive regard. Or it would stand in the way of my empathy. It could, in the sense of my not being able to feel completely their pain.

Carmen's clients are likely aware of her physical discomfort, without her having to verbalise it. Her condition, when it is active, means that she 'struggles' when she walks or climbs the stairs leading to her office. Her clients, then, may have it more in the foreground of their minds than she does herself:

> They could visibly see [that I was in pain] … but I think when it's a chronic condition, you're not always aware that its sort of there all the time, sort of like part of the wallpaper … that's the norm … And then when I was at my worst, you'd have good days and bad days, but often the good days, there was just that chronic background pain.

Although Carmen tried to arrange periods away to coincide with her usual summer break, and she cut down on her workload generally, she was sometimes forced to take additional time out for treatment. She also found that following the last round of hospitalisation her mood plummeted:

> I went through a period of depression after yet another bout of treatment because I came back and I suppose, naturally, I expected to suddenly find a new me and it took about six months before the effects of that treatment kicked in, so I actually got worse ... I was very, very depressed, and at the time, my clients were a sort of lifeline. I felt they really ... it was the one thing I could focus on to get me through.

Carmen describes her depression as a 'depletion' of energy:

> So having to muster the energy to be with my clients, would kind of crank me up enough. I'd get cranked up enough to be able to work, and I think that was possible because I didn't have too many clients. If I had had a full workload, I don't know how I would have managed.

And while she could 'crank up' the energy to work, she had little left for anything else, slumping after every session and needing to rest. But she also insists that her experience of physical pain has deepened her ability to understand the suffering of others:

> I had ideas about pain, I had a sort of concept of pain, which is different from the experience of pain, and the experience of pain is that it comes in and out. Sometimes it's unbearable, and lots of times it's bearable and I can still function, even when I have pain. Even though I sometimes think I can't function. So, I think those experiences of it being a bit fragmented, make me feel differently when I'm with someone who's in pain, and I think we are able, as humans, to put up with a lot of pain – a lot more – and I think that our training is [to understand] how we defend ourselves from [psychological] pain ... and of course, so much of our work is to learn to understand how we do this, so I think, you know, pain isn't so separate from our lives.

Pain in awareness

Carmen is linking the tangible elements of physical pain, if you like, with the often indefinable qualities of emotional pain. As therapists, we are also often conscious that patients 'somatise', expressing their internal distress through physical discomfort, pain and illness. In cases of deep repression, it simply has nowhere else to go, like rain dropping on already saturated ground, it must travel and find a way through somehow, often flooding us with physical symptoms such as backaches, skin conditions and bad colds. And it doesn't stop there: a client trapped in a job he disliked found that his hands became paralysed. At the point he was about to be operated on, he decided to quit and pursue a quieter life as an artist. Almost instantly he began to feel some movement, and over a period of months his hands gradually came back to life. This isn't a miracle, but rather the final release of some internal pressure previously too great to bear.

Carmen also raises an interesting question when she speaks of holding her pain 'in awareness'. Rather than 'bracketing' the pain, or attempting to shove it underground, acknowledgement of the pain, at least to ourselves, may be a way of managing the experience in the room. So often in our work as counsellors and therapists, we are confronted by clients who diminish their suffering, who play down the cost of previous physical and psychological abuse through a regular discounting of current experience. In the case of these patients and clients, everyone else's suffering is worse than theirs. They push themselves beyond endurance, because as children they were often forced to do so.

This may not be a question of self-disclosure to our clients; it is an acknowledgement to ourselves that we are struggling. I believe that whatever we bring into the therapy room becomes part of the relationship between us, unconscious or otherwise. We may like to imagine that we can keep the sharper elements of our daily lives out of the room, but they are forever with us – like death and taxes, ultimately unavoidable. Pain, too, can only be made to work *for* us if it is acknowledged.

Working with pain

Among the therapists I spoke to during my research, a quarter of them had experienced serious or chronic illnesses in the course of their working lives, and another suffered an accident in which he nearly died. Although the illness in every case had passed or gone into remission, and the cuts and broken bones had healed, the wounds were still raw. Pain may be universal, but the experience is individual and each therapist managed in their own way. For some there was a 'need' to work, while others were forced to take time out, whether they wanted to or not. Carmen's need to work does illustrate how employment is often our most effective refuge during times of stress.

Gawande (2003) points out that physical experiences such as pain 'are conceived as "neuromodules" in the brain ... Pain is a symphony – a complex response that includes not just a distinct sensation but also motor activity, a change in emotion, a focusing of attention, a brand-new memory' (p. 125). Nor, he says, is it constant, ebbing and flowing as it does, interacting within a complex structure of emotion and circumstance: 'Pain that doesn't arise from physical injury is no less real than pain that does – in the brain it is exactly the same' (p. 129).

While writing this chapter I visited a close friend and colleague who had recently undergone a hip replacement operation. The pain of recovery was intense, and lasted far longer than she had anticipated, forcing her to take more time out. 'But when a client rang, and I had to speak to them, I forgot the pain for a while,' she said. 'It was just lovely, but afterwards the pain was even worse because I hadn't been paying attention to my body. I had stiffened up.' During the night, when there were no distractions, the pain was at its most intense. This in turn left her exhausted, less able than ever to manage both the physical and emotional repercussions of her operation.

My colleague's experience on the phone with her clients is replicated throughout therapy rooms everywhere, to greater or lesser degrees. Even if Carmen has found a way to settle into a rhythm with her pain, accepting it as the backdrop to her life, others are persecuted with anything from chronic arthritis, to a toothache (which can be formidable!) and the annoyance of stinging eyes during a spring bout of hay fever. Even the slightest headache can prove distracting. A strained muscle from an early morning run or a game of weekend tennis can make sitting in our therapy chair uncomfortable. Recovering from an operation, even months later, can still cause us pain. All can be experienced as torment, and all may be relieved through the distraction of working with clients and patients.

For those of us who are accustomed to good health, or assume that we are 'healthy' and someone who 'simply doesn't get sick', the onset of illness or a disability can be crushing. It interferes with our sense of self, in the Rogerian sense, our 'self concept' (Rogers, 1967). When pain or illness arrives, this may constitute a painful, internal process of reorganising the 'self' to accommodate this new, more vulnerable 'me'. This may be particularly difficult for therapists, many of whom consider themselves 'copers', people who have struggled through difficult histories and emerged the other end fit and well and psychologically solid enough to become therapists themselves.

Case study: the loss of invincibility

Wallace is a CBT therapist, working in a busy mental health clinic in Canada. He is a big man, solid and perhaps to some people intimidating due to his size and evident strength. No one would suppose that he is a man recovering from a deep psychological wound brought on by an injury made more difficult due to the onset of age. Wallace is in his fifties and at one time was a professional hockey player, an occupation that carries with it god-like status in Canada. However, this was also an era before players received daunting amounts of money and when his hockey career ended he had to find work, initially training as a social worker. For many years he worked with teenagers, often coaching local community teams. He never gave up his own skating either, at least once a week joining mates for a 'friendly', usually at midnight when they could get rink time. At the age of forty, and through his work as a social worker, he was offered the opportunity to train as a therapist and he grabbed at it.

Like most professional, or experienced, athletes, Wallace saw pain as part of the game; the amount of suffering endured often considered a point of personal pride. Skating, running or playing through an injury is not unheard of among sportsmen and women, where pushing through pain 'barriers' in order to win is the norm, rather than the exception. For many athletes pain is actually seen as a virtue, an indicator that they are working hard. Wallace, not surprisingly, had a view of himself as physically invincible. He may have had to give up his professional career, but he never gave up hockey and into his late forties, working as a therapist, he suddenly faced a crisis following an injury to his leg during a game. For months he discounted it, not even taking medical advice. He continued to walk, though a little stiffly, and he tried to ignore the almost constant throbbing. Although back at work for over a year, the experience was still very alive for Wallace when he spoke to me, even using the present tense to describe the effect of his injury:

> For a long period of time, I mean this has been going on for nine months, but I've actually been in pain all of that time, and I've always taken a quite cavalier approach to pain. I played hockey for 40 years and it was always, oh it'll be alright in a few weeks, but it got to the point where I was sitting in this very chair and I could hear every single noise outside, the doors banging, people talking, noise is a problem, but you do adjust to it.

Wallace realised that his hyper-sensitivity was a symptom of a greater problem. His cavalier approach towards physical pain was no longer working. He was in a state of hyper-arousal, such as people experience after trauma:

> And I think that's how I was and I realised something was wrong and I went off sick straight away, and during that period, that's when I went

to seek some sort of therapy. And one of the things that came to my attention through the therapy sessions was that I've always had that ... almost like a cavalier approach to life. I've brushed off everything that's ever happened to me, and never really dealt with it, and seen myself as invincible, and this particular injury, because the pain hadn't gone within a few weeks, and because I hadn't adopted the patient role, it sort of crept up on me.

Wallace was faced in therapy with more than simply an adjustment to pain and an acceptance that his injury was more serious than he had considered: his whole sense of self was challenged:

I think the time was right when I think probably I was at a crossroads in my life anyway, but it was quite a fertile time to undergo therapy. But it was sort of enforced because, you know, I recognised something was wrong at work which had never happened before, and I did feel sort of duty bound to do something about it. I wasn't quite sure what was going on, but I knew it had something to do with pain and with maybe not adapting or giving into it, not adopting a sicker role.

Wallace is a CBT therapist and so therapy was never mandated during his training, something he believes should now be introduced. However, he did opt for therapy at this time of deep internal conflict when he recognised that something was wrong, something more than the physical injury itself (Jones, 1997). He also opted for a humanistic therapist, rather than a practitioner reflecting his own cognitive behavioural training. This does not indicate a lack of faith in the tradition in which he practises, but simply recognition that at particular times, and for specific personal difficulties, one approach may be better suited than another.

Wallace also discovered, when he returned to work a few months later, that a client had registered an informal complaint against him, which disturbed him greatly. His understanding is that she felt abandoned when he took his extended leave, 'and she wanted some kind of redress, perhaps'. However, he also asks himself whether the pain he was experiencing, the extent of which he was unable to acknowledge even to himself at the time, interfered with his ability to empathise:

I keep going back over the time and I think, well, did this ... maybe did the pain affect my performance, because my client actually had problems with pain – constant headaches – and I'm thinking well, did I ever identify with her pain?

Coping: admission and recovery

As Wallace illustrates, therapists are often 'survivors', which I consider in Chapter 6 when I focus on personal histories. However, the notion of 'coping' also has significance here where therapists admit to impatience, or working beyond the moment when they, and arguably their patients, might have benefited from their taking a break (Gold and Nemiah, 1993). How are we to know when we can work through our pain, as in Carmen's case, or not, as in Wallace's? And finally, work for many therapists has proved a welcome refuge from the pain and suffering of their own lives, sometimes to the benefit of their clients, and sometimes not, leaving us with the difficult question: how do we tell the difference?

Winifred, by her own admission, is a 'coper'. When she learned that she had breast cancer and needed surgery, she did not close up shop immediately. Rather, she did not tell anyone and she continued working. Her son, as it happened, was graduating from university in a few weeks' time, a source of enormous pride to him and the rest of the family as he is dyslexic and academic studies had always been very difficult for him. Winifred did not want to deprive him of the pure pleasure of his accomplishment through worry about her. In order to play out the fantasy, she also had to continue working, holding her own counsel and letting no one in on the secret in case they became preoccupied with her health too:

> I didn't stop work and I didn't tell any of the family because I didn't want the graduation to be spoilt. I tried to look after myself and when the graduation was over obviously everybody knew and were able to help. There was that element, you know, that's my [internal] message – 'you'll be alright, keep strong!'

Following the graduation, she had the operation immediately and, although she did not have to undergo chemotherapy, she did return to work rather quickly:

> Two weeks later I was back at work and that was foolish, foolish, because any loss, any bereavement, whatever it is, you've gotta grieve for, and so I think you are most probably right. My clients missed out.

Would she do the same thing again? Perhaps a longer break following the operation, but regarding her son's graduation, she is not sure. 'I don't know what you do,' she said, 'I don't know. Very difficult that one.'

Part of our struggle as therapists is our ability to rationalise our behaviour. Just as our clients do, we find a way sometimes to continue doing what we want to do, exchanging the word *want* for *need* and even going one further, convincing ourselves that our clients can't do without us, upping our own value in the process. If we are indispensable we then *must* be important. We *want* to continue working, to relieve our own anxiety perhaps, or to distract us from pain.

The legacy of life-threatening illness

Saul is a psychoanalytic therapist who also faced a diagnosis of cancer several years ago. The notion of suddenly being ill had an 'enormous impact' on him. Saul had part of his bowel removed as a result of the diagnosis:

> It's really had a profound effect in the sense that I think, you know, everything should go well, and perhaps it will, one doesn't know ... but the idea that life is finite and so the loss for me is I guess that I'm invincible and will live forever.

However, even a few years later, within the therapy room there is still a physical legacy of that time. With patients he often sits as he did with me, with his arms crossed, holding himself in such a way as if to protect his abdomen, that part of himself where he imagines he has lost a section of his bowel. He is very aware that there is less of him now than there was before the operation, even if he is more readily able to express an appreciation for the finite qualities of life. 'I think I've become much more aware that time is precious and how do I want to spend my time and what I want to do with my time, and those kinds of things.' As a result, Saul has cut back on some of his committee duties, an aspect of his career development he found torturous. Instead he has taken up playing the cello again, an instrument he played as a child. He is taking regular lessons and meeting up with other musicians to develop his skills, an activity he finds far more satisfying and 'balancing'.

The return to work

Early in my first training as a counsellor, while still in my clinical placement, I was travelling abroad and fell ill with pneumonia. After several weeks in hospital in South Africa, I returned home. Unable to stay awake for longer than a few hours without a nap, I was forced to take time out. When my energy finally did return I was left with a lingering cough. It was ugly and rasping and sounded worse than it actually felt. I went back to work.

I was very inexperienced and told none of my clients what had happened, though I was noticeably thinner, certainly paler, and I couldn't stop the coughing.

I had only a few clients at the time, one of whom narrowed her eyes when she sat down, but asked me nothing about where I'd been or what had happened to me. With every cough her forehead furrowed a little more deeply. I know now I should have queried her expression, or reflected it back to her. This would have opened up the possibility for discussion, and a consideration of what personal meaning my illness held for her. Instead, I blithely carried on, about which I remember nothing. I believe now that I was not so afraid of what my illness might mean for her, so much as I was afraid of what it might mean for me. I wanted to be well, to carry on with my studies.

Another client was angry, exhorting me to have an x-ray and demanding that I tell her whether or not I had consulted a doctor. For some reason I was able to respond appropriately, probably because the state of my health was being openly acknowledged. Her anger didn't diminish – I was clearly eliciting an archaic response in the context of parental neglect and alcoholism – and she needed me to look after myself so that I could look after her, and when she imagined I was not, she became furious. However, as her focus on my health was so clearly rooted in her past, I was again able to side-step the question of my readiness to return to work. In other words, while we explored my client's history, I could avoid the 'here and now' issue of my own health and the reasons why I had elicited such a deeply felt disturbance in her.

Lasky (1990) speaks of having to consider his own illness in light of his patient's concern regarding his health. He argues that regardless of whether or not we disclose the details of our illness, our condition will impact on our patients. Pizer writes of 'working with patients while working with a life-threatening, body-altering illness' (1998, p. 193). She speaks of the 'elephant in the room', around which self-disclosure is 'inescapable'. In Pizer's case, she was forced to take additional time out to undergo and recuperate from a mastectomy, and as a result of the chemotherapy she began to lose her hair, one of the more obvious side effects of her illness. In her moving treatise on the loaded meaning of the 'breast' in psychoanalytic terms, she says:

> While the analyst's awareness of uncertainty or anxiety will most likely be communicated to her patients, these raw states – as states in themselves – are problematic when either denied or directly 'bled' out into the room. The analyst must find some words to explain and contain these affects, although not necessarily in concrete informational form. For both persons, the stark exposure of the analyst's anxiety surges – specifically about her cancer – can be a mutually destabilizing force that undermines the analytic process in a variety of ways (e.g., the patient may flee, deny his senses, or attempt to take care of his analyst):

Thus, each analyst must remain attentive and connected to her own sense of how stable she can remain in the face of her uncertainties, how grounded and prepared she is to deal with whatever surprises of affect or inquiry may arise. My own choice to disclose my illness to patients grows out of who I am as a person and who I am as a practising clinician.

(Pizer, 1998, pp. 196–197)

I believe that if we, as therapists, are holding up a mirror to our patients, it's pretty convenient if we allow it to shine only one way, avoiding what we might see in ourselves. And it is far too easy to dismiss a client's uncomfortable suggestion that we may have returned to work too soon, or that we are avoiding certain areas of discussion as simply aspects of the transference, so nothing to do with us. This is simply denying the power of our own defences, which despite years of therapy in many cases, will certainly be reactivated during times of stress and illness. As Lasky points out, when we are ill we are also likely to regress into 'infantilism' (1990, p. 464) becoming for a period of time the focus of everyone's concern. Giving that up to return to the robust requirements of the therapy room where the needs of our patients are paramount, is hard work.

Conclusion

Taking refuge in our work is entirely human. However, do we as therapists have a responsibility not to 'use' our clients to ease our pain, any more than a mother should not 'use' her child to defend and soothe herself against the stresses of her personal life? As we so often learn from our clients and patients in the therapy room, this shift in the order of a child's reliance on mother, can often lead to future difficulties for the 'adult' child (Stern, 1985).

This is not to say we should not work, but rather we must consider the question. Carmen courageously holds her pain 'in awareness', struggling everyday with a chronic condition. This enables her to empathise most of the time, but when the suffering is too intense, by her own admission she closes off. Through a denial of his own vulnerability, Wallace suffered the consequences, obliged to take time out in the end. Like the ancient warrior, Philoctetes – stranded on his island through shame of his wound – he was forced, ultimately, to return to the world with a more human view of himself. Winifred 'coped', but regrets returning to work too soon, and Saul has made changes to his life as a result of his illness. These therapists are not exceptions; they could be any one of us at some point in our working lives as therapists. Pain is universal, but how we manage it is individual.

4 Black dog

Therapists' depression

Depression is both completely concrete and entirely intangible, for many people even beyond the possibility of description. In *Darkness Visible*, William Styron writes of the inadequacy of the word 'depression', a 'true wimp of a word' he says, which has 'slithered innocuously through the language like a slug, leaving little trace of its intrinsic malevolence and preventing, by its very insipidity, a general awareness of the horrible intensity of the disease when out of control' (1990, p. 37). While some therapists are still able to 'function' while depressed, for others the experience is so bleak and debilitating they must take a break from seeing clients. Those clinicians, as Styron says, 'have endured despair beyond despair' (p. 84).

Winston Churchill called depression his 'Black Dog' (Storr, 1990, p. 84), and Andrew Solomon refers to it as the *Noonday Demon* (2001) in his brilliant study of his own and others' experience of depression. Bessie Smith sang of her 'empty bed blues', waking up in the morning with an 'awful aching head'. Euripides writes of Electra, that her 'cheeks bleed silently', an evocation of relentless suffering stemming, in her case, from unbearable guilt and loss. From the ancient to the contemporary, depression in all its forms is expressed. It is forever with us, from the mournful taste of a single day that may evoke a previous heartbreak, to the ongoing struggle to move through one day into the next one, surviving and waking up with an 'awful aching head'.

The word 'depression' is often used as a kind of shorthand for a state of disenchantment that can range from a low level rumbling of a general dissatisfaction with our lives in the moment, and which we often work hard to cover up through frenetic activity, shopping, or self-medication, to the abyss of suffering which we cannot ever imagine finding a way out of, the only option sometimes appearing to be suicide. As Darian Leader suggests, depression may be as 'varied as those who are told that they suffer from it'. There are as many forms as there are people afflicted, without any easy tag or definition, 'more akin to states like fever: they might look the same across a wide range of people but their causes will be quite diverse' (2008, pp. 17, 18).

The numbers

Following the death of two prominent psychologist practitioners in the United States, the American Psychological Association established a committee to investigate the prevalence of suicide among its members. They concluded that, along with other health care workers, there was evidence to suggest an 'elevated' risk of suicide greater than in the general population (Kleespies *et al.*, 2011). Of the forty clinicians I spoke to, twenty-two told me they had experienced depression since qualifying as therapists. Among those, fifteen participants said their depression was 'episodic', for instance due to illness or the onset of a general dissatisfaction with life in the moment. The remaining therapists described their condition as chronic, having struggled with depression for much of their lives.

Depression is an area where therapists did show differences according to tradition. While under half of psychoanalytic therapists admitted they had suffered depression since beginning work, over three-quarters of the integrative therapists and nearly three-quarters of humanistic therapists said they had also had to cope with depression. Half of CBT therapists were affected.

These numbers also echo Pope and Tabachnick's study (1994), where 61 per cent of the 500 therapists they questioned reported experiencing depression, with a full 29 per cent of these contemplating suicide. In fact, 4 per cent had actually tried to kill themselves. If these numbers reflect something of our community as a whole, it also means that there is a higher rate of depression among therapists than there is within the general population. According to the UK Office for National Statistics, just over 9 per cent of the population in Britain experience anxiety or depression at any one time, which breaks down to nearly 5 per cent suffering depression and nearly 3 per cent struggling with anxiety. Under 2 per cent of the population experience a combination of anxiety and depression (Office of National Statistics, 2000). In 2010 there were 5,608 confirmed suicides in people 15 years and over in the UK, 17.0 per 100,000 for men and 5.3 per 100,000 for women (Office of National Statistics, 2012).[1] Estimates of depression over a lifetime vary from between one in six to one in four (Bird, 1999), according to the Mental Health Foundation. It also predicts that by the year 2020 'depression' will be the second most common cause of disability, after heart disease.

That therapists are prone to depression is not such a surprise if we believe that our histories contribute to our becoming therapists, which I discuss in Chapter 6. For instance, of the twenty-two therapists in this study who have experienced depression, more than half of those suffered a form of abandonment as children including alcoholism, death of a parent and divorce. Significantly, only three therapists who experienced abandonment of this nature in childhood did not experience depression; one psychoanalytic therapist linked his emotional containment to an ability to reach out to others:

> I don't get depressed. I'm pretty resourceful in that way. I do what I advise my clients to do, use your network of support, don't get isolated, so it's a bit of a catch-22 for people that when they start to get in a low mood and a bit depressed, they close themselves off, and they lose a real buffer against mental ill health which is connection with other people.

But not everyone is as lucky as Raymond, with an ability to push beyond the iron curtain of depression to find a way out. Like the general population, therapists facing a debilitating form of the illness find it as difficult as anyone else to break loose and reach out – sometimes because they cannot, though sometimes too, perhaps, because they will not, experiencing deep shame or fear of rejection at the prospect of others knowing of their vulnerability. Penny is an integrative therapist, her experience a case in point:

> I talked to a colleague whom I expected to be quite understanding, and I was absolutely shocked! There was absolutely nothing there, and that's what scared me, that this was my problem. I found that quite difficult ... knowing that she was a therapist and her reaction was that it was almost something I was imagining ... It was quite shocking. It was as if you were having a conversation with somebody and they almost get up and come and slap you across the face, you know, that unexpected and that shocking.

As Penny spoke her eyes grew wide and she looked terrified, as if expecting me to slap her too. Clearly she does not anticipate support from those she works with. Penny is not afraid of admitting she is vulnerable, she is only frightened of admitting it within her own community!

The front line experience

> Some part of me instinctively reached out, and in an odd way understood this pain, never imagining that I would someday look in the mirror and see their sadness and insanity in my own eyes.
>
> (Jamison, 1996, p. 25)

Are we, as therapists, attracted to the profession *because* of our history of depression, or are we more vulnerable to depression and anxiety due to our constant exposure to human distress, sometimes experiencing 'vicarious trauma'? Clearly, therapists are not immune from what may be the 'disease' of the age, 'melancholia' as it was once more commonly known (Freud, 1917).

As I have already highlighted, depression can mean many things to different people, and even within the therapeutic community there are differences of interpretation. At one end of the spectrum therapists were clearly speaking of what might be referred to as the 'blues', while others talked of a completely debilitating experience when they were actually unable to function, losing all perspective and sight of reality.

The word 'depression' seems to surface to describe a prolonged period of despondency and hopelessness, when therapists are faced with experiences in their lives which are apparently out of their control, sometimes, but not always, triggered by current events such as redundancy, illness or death. Like so many of our clients, helplessness evokes powerful feelings of despair.

However, with such a discrepancy between the traditions, I also wonder at the self-disclosing nature of those who choose to train in one tradition or another. Humanistic therapists, for instance, hold congruence and authenticity true to their professional hearts (Rogers, 1959), while psychoanalytic psychotherapists are usually discouraged from self-disclosure (Racker, 1968). A number of contemporary therapists, such as Maroda (2004), advocate some disclosure of their feelings concerning the patient, but this is a recent shift in belief within the community. How likely, then, are psychoanalytic therapists to admit such vulnerability? However, the psychoanalytic psychotherapists I spoke to *did* open up, often revealing deeply meaningful histories of pain and distress, though 'grief' and 'loss' were more likely to be named, rather than 'depression', such as in the case of Alice and her sorrow over not having children (Chapter 2).

Within the psychoanalytic community the general ennui of life is taken as a given with Freud's notion of 'hysterical misery turned into common unhappiness', perhaps reflecting to some degree those therapists' personal view of the world (Breuer and Freud, 1895, p. 305). However, the more American right to the 'pursuit of happiness'[2] may be engendered into the training of other traditions where members of the humanistic community may have a looser definition of 'depression'. If we are not happy, are we then 'depressed'? For cognitive therapists, certainly the diminishing of symptoms might be interpreted as bringing about relief and less reason to be depressed, if not actually promoting the idea of 'happiness'. And how debilitated do we need to become to be diagnosed as 'depressed'?

Case study: taking time out

Max is a therapist working in the heart of Glasgow. He has a busy private practice and also, until a year ago, ran a counselling service in Edinburgh, on a good day with little traffic, about an hour's drive away. He loves his city and he loves his job as a therapist, but Max has also suffered three bouts of depression during the period he's been working. His illness manifested as a 'depletion of energy' both 'spiritually and emotionally'.

The first time Max experienced depression he took a break of six weeks, and on the second he remained off work for eight weeks. During both these periods he returned to therapy, which he found very useful and he credits with helping him emerge into health again. But, for Max, it was his third bout of depression which proved most meaningful. He was forced to take a total of four months off, during which he also had to take stock of his life. Three months into his depression, and about to return to work, he went to see the psychiatrist monitoring his medication:

> He said, in the kind of work that you do, you need to be sharp, you need to be on the ball. Up until that point, I was feeling terribly responsible and shameful and letting my clients down and all that kind of stuff, that I'm sure I'm not Robinson Crusoe. So when he said, don't go back until you're sharp and you're back into it, I was really relieved about that.

But making a decision not to work is a difficult one, particularly for those therapists who are self-employed. But, says Max, what was even more frightening was his lack of fear. Depression, he says overrode even his ability to be frightened of losing everything in his life. He was 'relieved' at the doctor's suggestion that he take more time out and didn't return to work for another month. Nor did he return to therapy during this period. Instead, he changed his life:

> Once I started to function and the medication kicked in a bit more, and once I kind of thought about my life a bit more, I really felt that the depression this time, on the third occasion, was really a gift, to help me look at my life and the kind of lifestyle I was leading ... At that stage I was the manager of a counselling service, doing 60+ hours a week, plus the commute. I wasn't really looking after myself terribly well. I gave that job up. I started a meditation programme. I started to really take care of myself.

Max also had a difficult home life. Although he was reluctant to let go of his marriage, he was also aware that the relationship 'wasn't great'. A few months after his full recovery and his return to work, his wife left him:

> Despite the separation being a very traumatic experience, it didn't stop my capacity to function. I was able to get up each day and, you know,

get my breakfast and go to work and drive and do all the things that one would normally do, maybe with a background sense of sadness, but it didn't actually stop me functioning, whereas the depression did … that really was the stark difference.

For Max, despite the debilitating nature of his depression, and the fear associated with his possible loss of income and his struggles within his marriage, he was able to use his extended leave to make solid and productive changes to his lifestyle, something he believes he would not have done had he returned to work a month earlier. During that period he might have been able to work, but he would not have changed his life, making it more likely that the depression would return. He believes that it was because he implemented these changes that he felt 'sadness' at the end of his marriage, rather than 'depression'. He could, in his words, 'function'.

Max also believes that his experience has enabled him to work more empathically with clients suffering depression. However, he adds:

> I'm also aware that my journey out and through depression is not necessarily the same journey for everyone. So even though it gives me a greater empathy … it still has challenges when it's experienced in other people. So even though I don't get pulled into the vortex, I still from time to time feel a challenge working with depressed clients.

Managing the experience

Anxiety is my usual response to life's inevitable difficulties, though there have also been days when, in my vernacular, I have felt 'depressed', with a much lower energy threshold than normal. Perhaps I have been lucky, because so many of my colleagues have had to struggle through much darker periods, and over long periods of time. This doesn't mean I am immune; only that my time may not yet have arrived. I now also believe that my anxiety is sometimes a defence against depression, motivating me forward in an attempt to keep going, a defence against death, if you like (Chapter 5). Many of the therapists I spoke to who suffered episodic bouts rather than chronic depression were surprised by their experience, sometimes not even recognising the early signs. Hanford, an integrative psychotherapist, works both in private practice and within a psychiatric, high security hospital in the British Midlands. His depression was unexpected, and completely unfamiliar to him:

> What I noticed first of all was that everything was starting to be a bit of a blur. I was noticing that I became anxious – anxiety was my biggest

symptom – but not [when I was] sitting with clients … then it started to creep into other areas of my work at the hospital.

Teaching became impossible and he began dreading seeing even his private clients, who were technically not so psychologically disturbed as those he saw at the hospital. Despite Hanford's anxiety levels ratcheting higher each day, and receiving a diagnosis of 'clinical depression', he continued working until he was 'forced' to stop:

> Because it's the first time I've ever become depressed, there was a bit of me – probably an omnipotent part of me – that thought I can cope, I can cope and certainly that was a huge learning curve for me.

Following Hanford's initial struggle to admit he was 'ill', he finally took help in the form of medication as well as therapy. The medication did not appear to have any effect and his ongoing therapy, in the humanistic tradition, also seemed to have hit a wall. Much to his surprise, it was CBT therapy he found most useful during his depression. Like Wallace (Chapter 3), he discovered that *this* kind of therapy at *this* particular juncture suited him best. Afterwards he returned to long-term therapy, working with a Jungian analyst.

However, the consequences were far-reaching and Hanford was forced to take leave on health grounds twice. Finally returning to work at the hospital, he initially concentrated on other duties, choosing not to see clients again for two years.

The peril of abrupt endings

One of the consequences of refusing to attend to ourselves and our moods may be that ultimately we let our clients down far harder than had we admitted our vulnerability much earlier.

Finishing with clients is not simple, and if the ending is sudden it can be damaging to our clients and patients, perhaps evoking archaic traumatic experiences. In the previous chapter we heard from Wallace, reflecting on his difficult experience with clients when he ended the relationship unexpectedly due to his leg injury. One client actually resorted to a complaint. Hanford also admits that for the months leading up to his break he was working on 'automatic pilot' and ultimately the ending with his clients was far too abrupt.

Throughout my study, therapists repeated that they felt they had not taken enough time out during personal crises. Mark also continued to work with patients while 'depressed', in his case within a health service about to face closure. He now believes that this was damaging, admitting that he was 'distracted' with clients and unable to attend to them appropriately while he was so preoccupied with his own concerns. He was also not sleeping or eating 'properly' and struggled with acute anxiety throughout that period, his exhaustion also no doubt contributing to his inability to attend to his clients as attentively as he would normally.

One CBT therapist connected his low-level, chronic depression with his early history, including a mother with a severe psychiatric illness. Describing himself as a 'functional depressive' he admitted there were periods when he dipped below 'functioning' level, and was 'running on empty a bit', his symptoms sometimes echoing those of his clients with, 'early morning wakings and stuff like that'.

Wanda, a humanistic therapist, has been prone to depression for many years. She also knows the signs, the marked slide in both her mood and energy levels, which tell her that she is moving into a period of depression. This means she can take a measured approach, building in breaks and ensuring that she feels fit to work. The most she has taken off is two weeks, but she says categorically, 'I would be very clear about not working if I was really unwell, but do continue to work when I'm under par.'

Looking for love?

Solomon equates depression with a forsaking of 'love' and when we believe we have been so forsaken, we believe only that we are 'insignificant' (2001, p. 15). We are, in essence, left without any sense of meaning, a profound existential crisis that logically might lead to suicide. In *Why Love Matters*, Gerhardt (2004) points out that the children of depressed mothers are about six times more likely to suffer depression themselves, children with a sense of having been 'forsaken'. Of the twenty-two therapists who spoke to me of their depression, more than half of them as children had suffered some form of parental abandonment.

Do we then remain working, not just to distract us from the acute suffering of depression, but also to find a way back to 'love', through our clients' appreciation of our skills, our attendance to them, our constancy? Under these circumstances we are deluding ourselves, and perhaps hurting our patients. Through depression we can instead be emotionally absent and at risk of replicating earlier, traumatic abandonment, made worse through our delay in admitting we need to take a break. And in embracing the most tragic aspects of grandiosity, we may sometimes mistake appreciation for what we do, with the more profound experience of being 'loved' for who we are.

Sandra says that 'I'm probably constantly depressed', which she believes interferes 'only intermittently with her work'. She regularly gives herself 'sick days' when she is not feeling well and admits that sometimes her 'depression' is drug and alcohol induced. Sometimes she 'just goes to the doctor' and has them sign her off sick 'for a couple of weeks'. Aside from two sessions of relationship counselling, Sandra has never experienced personal therapy, a paradox I find difficult to accept. 'I probably should have,' she said, 'but I just don't think it would work for me.' Her view was echoed by another therapist who refused to return to therapy as she knows all the 'tricks'.

It is my belief that grandiosity is a defence against feeling small. It can also manifest itself in myriad ways, including the notion that we are 'beyond' the help of therapy. Why, for instance, would you believe that therapy can provide support and insight to others, but not work for you, a therapist?

Oscar, a psychoanalytic therapist, has episodically experienced periods of depression. He says it is the one thing that would drive him back into therapy, but only if the depression became so intense that he became, in his words, 'ill':

> I think it would be depression. I mean ... no I've never been incapacitated for weeks, but I can certainly remember times during intense experiences when I was working with borderline people. You would go through a couple of weeks when you weren't very productive, you know, which I think could equally have been labelled depression. Though not the kind that takes root and limits things. I mean ... Yeah, I can remember, yeah, four years ago, when I cut down my work quite significantly for six months. I felt I just needed to get away and I think that's the very end of the line. Would I go into therapy again? I probably wouldn't unless I had a kind of, you know, something approaching an illness, which I couldn't manage.

Like Sandra, Oscar may be struggling with an admission that he is vulnerable, as if he cannot take help for himself until he is actually ill, by then quite a long way down the road of depression. This raises the question, why not seek therapy earlier? However, if shame is lurking behind any admission that he might need help, or he does not trust that his colleagues will be supportive, as in Penny's case, he is certainly unlikely to ask for help earlier.

Anthea is a psychotherapist who works at the cognitive end of the integrative spectrum. She says she suffers depression 'regularly' and has done so for much of her life, certainly since she was a teenager. There are times when she can connect her 'depression' to a particular loss or event, such as her partner's illness, but that is not always necessarily the case. She would not return to therapy as she doesn't believe it can work for her, ' ...

so I just go on anti-depressants'. She has never taken leave from her clinical work as a result of depression, although there are mornings when she finds the prospect of seeing clients difficult:

> when I wake up in the morning, I'm thinking oh God, oh God, I've got to get ready for work, you know, I hope nobody's too depressed! But actually, when it comes, when I'm in the room with the client, that goes and, umm, I'm ... you know, then it's like a different space.

Anthea believes she can 'split off' her experience of depression when working with clients, though, by her own admission, she is 'great at denial'. Another therapist suffering depression admitted that he does not 'trust' therapists – the only therapist he trusts, he says, is himself.

Do as I say not as I do

Therapy can dig out the roots of experience, which can often be painful. In my view, in order to avoid pain, these therapists may be prolonging their suffering, by not wanting to walk through that ring of fire, revisiting old experiences which may prove to have been smouldering for years. What else is 'depression' but a symptom of distress, a warning that something is simmering underneath? Therapy cannot do away with suffering, but it may help us to manage it, and therapists have, at the very least, an ethical responsibility to give it a try. Why would Sandra or Anthea believe that therapy works for others, when it cannot work for them? This may be a grandiose position, indicating that they believe they are above the norm where the therapeutic process might help. But if grandiosity is simply the means to avoid our own humanity, to ensure that we remain above others, then this may be indicative of the need for some therapeutic work as well, or at least some kind of reality check. What is Sandra's drug and alcohol use, so severe that it evokes 'depression', if not an effort to self-soothe? It is my position that we are all human, we are all vulnerable, and as therapists we all need to give ourselves a try in therapy before we impose it on anyone else, to say nothing of actually making a living out of it.

Psychotherapy may not be about 'cure' so much as it is about 'insight' and containment; some way of managing our internal crisis. So, for us to deny ourselves the very containment we offer our clients will verge, again, on the unethical. Certainly it is not good practice. Our expectations of what therapy is capable of delivering may also need to be reviewed: do we want/ expect a 'miracle' cure, a Lazarus-like lifting of the depression, or can we 'settle' for some understanding of its shape and history, some knowledge of how it impacts others, including our clients and patients?

Therapy as containment: when it does work?

Wynn believes that therapy has helped her to deal with a lifelong depression, resulting from a disturbing early history where both her parents suffered with mental health issues and her mother often expressed psychotic behaviour. She was in analysis for over ten years, through which she gained insight and understanding into her condition.

Despite her depression, Wynn has worked for many years as a therapist without taking time out. She credits her sense of duty, and the structure of her work as *enabling* her, rather than considering that her depression might *interfere* with her work. 'I have a very strong sense of responsibility,' she says. 'I'm not going to shut down in a depression – I'm just not going to do that – because that's been a survival mechanism, to be able to work, for better or worse.' Wynn believes that the structure of work and her focus on her commitment to her clients is what keeps her healthy. Along with her therapy, she credits collegial contact and regular, robust clinical supervision as the mainstays of her professional life.

Therapy, along with supervision, was often cited by therapists in the study as offering a 'lifeline' during difficult periods. Sharon is a case in point:

> That's my safeguard, my backstop. I don't always need it, and you know I've known my therapist a long time … I feel if I'm going to work as a therapist, I have to have my feet on the ground, so that I know that if there's something going on, I've got somewhere to take it, I've got somewhere to sort it. I don't have to worry too much about it.

Admitting we are vulnerable: a hazardous task?

As psychotherapists we counsel those who ask for help. So why are we, as a community, sometimes reluctant to seek out help ourselves?

I believe that there are often elements of shame connected with therapists having to seek therapeutic support – and even when we try to reach out, it may not always be forthcoming. While conducting research for this book I was speaking to a colleague and I mentioned the proportionally large number of therapists I spoke to who said they had suffered, or were currently suffering depression. 'They clearly shouldn't be working then,' she snapped. I was surprised at both the quickness, and the certainty with which she spoke, as if there was an absolute rule. What would she do, I wondered, if a therapist approached her for support? Would she be able to keep her judgemental attitude at bay? Surely she had also gone through rough times? In fact, I knew she had, with a personal life that included wayward children and a marriage that verged on a public sham. It struck me then that perhaps we can keep our own miseries at bay by avoiding the unhappiness in others, particularly our fellow therapists. Where is our compassion when it comes to them?

Penny, from whom we heard earlier, says there is a marked distinction between 'personal' and 'work-related' depression, for which she has received a great deal of support from colleagues. It was in the more deeply set, personal anguish that she felt so abandoned.

On the other hand, I also heard from therapists who spoke of the great support they received from colleagues while suffering depression, including Max, Wynn and Hanford. But there were a significant number who clearly found it difficult to ask for help, or who were disappointed when they did reach out, like Penny. I wonder how much we are defending ourselves against our personal vulnerability when we refuse to extend compassion towards our colleagues showing signs of *personal* vulnerability, rather than those evoked *through* the work: counter-transference responses, parallel processes and projections for instance.

And if we do not admit to ourselves that we are suffering, sometimes to the extent that it means we are functioning on 'automatic', we run a dreadful risk of harming ourselves further, and taking our clients down with us. We also perpetuate the 'myth' of the untroubled therapist, that we are superior in our ways of managing the world. In fact, we *are* more 'fortunate' than many in that we have knowledge. We actually have access to help, we know where to get it, and if the first therapist we make contact with isn't appropriate, we can move on to another who is a better 'fit'. It seems to me that those therapists who have the courage to move towards support, even in the midst of deep distress and fear, are those who are best equipped to see clients and patients. They understand the challenges, know and accept the limitations of psychotherapy. They also recognise the value of insight, of symbolising their anguish in words and thought to make meaning of their distress, thereby ensuring its manageability.

Therapy doesn't make depression go away, it simply provides leverage to face the day, to find a way through that 'despair beyond despair'. And it may not be a case that *if* we are facing pain in our personal life we should return to therapy, but *when*, the inevitable arriving once again at our door. It may be the very least we owe our clients.

Notes

1 This does not take into account 'narrative' verdicts from the coroner where 'some verdicts clearly state the intent and mechanism', for instance deaths from injury or poisoning must be coded as accidents. The ONS is obliged to code as suicide only those verdicts which are officially stated as such by

the coroner. 'Consequently, the net effect of the increase in narrative verdicts could potentially be to inflate the number of deaths classified as accidents and decrease the number classified as intentional self-harm' (Office of National Statistics 2012, p. 11).

2 'Life, Liberty and the Pursuit of Happiness', as written in the American Declaration of Independence.

5   Anxiety
Sparks flying upwards

Jessica was preparing to begin work for the afternoon when she clicked on her answer machine to hear her messages. Among the few from clients was also a request from the hospital that she ring them concerning her test results.

Six years before, Jessica had undergone a mastectomy. Since then she had faithfully attended her check-ups every six months, the last and final appointment just a few days previously. This was to be her all-clear, ending years of increasing anxiety leading up to every visit to the hospital. The moment Jessica heard the message she knew the cancer had returned. Why else would they ring?

She now had a decision to make. To ring the hospital, aware that if her suspicion was confirmed she would be too distressed to work, or delay calling back until after her last client of the day, knowing all the while what lay ahead. She opted to phone later, rather than cancel her patients at such short notice. By putting off that phone call she was also delaying the inevitable: 'It was a kind of surreal feeling that as long as I stayed in that room doing this work with this client, everything was alright.'

Reflecting on the experience so much later, she says that during those sessions, and despite her best efforts:

> It kept coming up. It was like a sort of sick feeling in my stomach that would just keep coming up and then it would go away, and then I would forget. I would get engrossed in the work and then the sick feeling would come again. I can remember looking at the clock a lot as well, thinking only 10 minutes, whereas normally I don't do that. You sort of look at the clock towards the end, but I kept looking at the clock, every sort of five or 10 minutes.

'A sort of sick feeling' and it 'would just keep coming up'. A conscientious therapist attempting to keep her anxiety at bay. If depression is a product of 'sorrow', or 'loss', either current or archaic, anxiety can be considered the other side of the coin, reflecting fear of the future (Mowrer, 1939; Solomon, 2001). The word 'stress' is often associated with the condition of current events, for instance the pressures of work, family stresses or, in extreme conditions, the threat of violence or war.

While therapists in my study spoke of their 'depression', they also articulated symptoms of anxiety: an inability to concentrate, restlessness and, for those therapists working in mental health settings, disenchantment and cynicism. In private practice, anxieties often concerned family members, ill health or financial worries. Sometimes anxiety was the *product* of depression, for others the flip side of depression, a hyper-activity to keep it at bay.

Anxiety: a physiological experience

Anxiety is often a visceral experience, as Jessica illustrates, and frequently beyond our control. Martin (1997) points out that psychological stress is so powerful it 'can induce physiological changes which may prove fatal to someone who already has a diseased heart or clogged coronary arteries' (pp. 3, 4). Most people don't literally drop down dead, but it can certainly make them 'more vulnerable to illness' (p. 32).

'Butterflies in my stomach', 'my heart sank', 'my heart started pounding', 'I broke out in a sweat', all of these sayings express the intensity of the 'anxious' or frightening experience. They aren't ideas, or simply handy metaphors, they are experiences, physiologically explicable, with shots of adrenaline coursing through the system. We clench our teeth, furrow our brows, bite our nails, bounce our knee up and down, fidget, and often struggle to concentrate – all of them signs of anxiety. And they interfere, like currents of electricity, between a client and his therapist. Even the most dedicated clinician can't beat nature when facing undue stress, their body sometimes expressing what their mind can't bear to hear.

Solomon, reflecting on his own experience, speaks of anxiety as inseparable from his depression, with one exacerbating the other. 'I experienced so much anxiety when I was depressed, and felt so depressed when I was anxious, that I came to understand the withdrawal and the fear as inseparable' (Solomon, 2001, p. 65).

In his presidential inaugural speech, Franklin D. Roosevelt said: 'The only thing we have to fear is fear itself – nameless, unreasoning, unjustified terror which paralyses needed efforts to convert retreat into advance' (1933). Sadly, of course, not all anxiety is unjustified, though the state itself can be unproductive. As Roosevelt highlights, anxiety can be inhibiting, often narrowing down a sense of life's possibilities. However, if that psychological paralysis can be pushed through, there may be an opening up and a sense of relief, the foundations of an emerging self-confidence. But actions can be destructive too. We see this all the time in our clients and patients, who come to us for some relief from their anxieties. There is no reason to assume that we are immune from paralysis ourselves, or the use of diversionary tactics to keep it at bay, such as drinking a little too much, or losing ourselves in our work at the expense of our family life. Boredom too, can evoke anxiety, the general ennui of life and disenchantment, the notion that there is 'nothing to do', or 'nothing we *can* do'.

Running for me is a means of self-regulation during periods of high anxiety. Writing also burns creative energy that helps to stem, or make sense of, that terrible 'visceral' anxiety that can verge on paralysis. The popular, and prolific, philosopher Alain de Botton has gone so far as to suggest that he hopes his children will not become writers (Stadien, 2010). The occupation, he says, is a product of anxiety, something from which he hopes they will be largely spared. An impossible hope, I suggest, though some people are obviously more prone than others.

Anxiety in my case invariably results in sleepless nights, which means I am less well equipped to deal with life in general, including clients. Sometimes, though, I am prompted to do something just to do anything that will grant me a sense of control again. And those kinds of actions are not thought out, they are impulse driven and often result in regret, in the end evoking additional anxiety. A dreadful, vicious circle.

The depression/anxiety matrix often echoes traumatic experience. If it happens once, it can happen again. On BBC Radio 4's programme *The Reunion* with Sue MacGregor (BBC, 2012), she was speaking to a group of Ugandan Asians forced to leave the country for Britain in 1972 when the dictator Idi Amin determined they were undermining the country's economy. They were allowed to leave with only what they could carry and £50 in their pocket. Years later one of the participants revealed that her mother still maintained they should always have a bag packed, just in case.

We do not have to suffer to this extent to understand that anxiety can undermine our sense of safety. Jessica's worst fear was manifest after the call from the hospital – the cancer had returned. A mother who loses a child is forever fearful that she will lose another; a therapist made redundant once knows that whatever service he joins may also close down. Therapists who face a complaint are acutely aware that it can happen again, unconsciously looking for signals that might indicate danger (Adams, 2008; Charles and Kennedy, 1985; Ferrell and Price, 1993; Kearns, 2007).

Recognising anxiety

Jessica's is an extreme example of anxiety interfering with work. Most of us don't have to be threatened with serious illness to evoke unease; sometimes it can be the ordinary demands of life such as raising kids, organising teaching, the pressure of external forces including ageing parents, mortgage payments, or an argument with your partner in the morning. Changes in our work patterns, the threat of redundancy, just about anything that interferes with life's usual rhythm, can lead to stress. For some people it can be the very predictability of life which leads to feelings of disenchantment and a sense of meaninglessness.

LeDoux distinguishes further between 'fear' and 'anxiety': 'Anxiety is usually distinguished from fear by the lack of an external stimulus that elicits the reaction – anxiety comes from within us, fear from the outside world' (1998, p. 228).

Referring back to the operation I underwent at nineteen (Chapter 3), the following day the anaesthetist paid me a visit. 'My goodness,' she said, 'You were *so* anxious. I was quite worried about you.' This was the first I knew about it. My father was a doctor, so hospitals didn't faze me – I used to go with him when he made his rounds, reading in the waiting room and watching the fish. Even now I find the smell of a hospital actually reassuring. My legs weren't bothering me much when I came into the hospital, and goodness knows I was pretty blasé about what lay ahead, superficially at least.

My point is we don't always recognise the extent of our unease. LeDoux points out that our brains light up like firecrackers even if we are not consciously aware of our anxiety. In my case, I had undergone minor operations in the past, and certainly my legs had caused me pain over the years. 'Emotional memories are not erased by extinction but are simply held in check. Extinguished memories, like Lazarus, can be called back to life' (LeDoux, 1998, p. 251).

Interestingly, he isn't saying anything therapists don't recognise in the course of their working lives. We *know* how memory and past trauma can play out in relationships, in self-sabotage and depression and anxiety; we see the evidence in our offices every day. What we may not consider so carefully is how our own anxieties play out in the therapy room. Caught between a rock and a hard place, Jessica tried hard to do well by her patients the day of the phone call, but she could not possibly have kept her terror in check. While dealing for many months with a complaint against me, I was not conscious of my anxiety, but it leaked through in my lack of spontaneity, in my hyper-sensitivity to particular clients and a general weariness resulting from restless nights and daytime tensions. And all the while I thought I was 'bracketing' it!

The age of anxiety

Every era is an 'age of anxiety' bringing with it particular stresses and strains. For those therapists working in New York after the attack on the Twin Towers, their anxiety was personal, echoing their own deep fear that it could happen again, even while they were caring for their patients in the same anguished state (Ragen, 2009). Therapists in Israel and Gaza equally struggle with day-to-day anxieties concerning the threat of violence and war. In New Zealand, following the Christchurch earthquake, therapists will not have been divorced from the terror that another 'big one' could strike again.

In retrospect, I realise that my therapist at the time of 9/11 was able to express a deep compassion for my dismay and horror through her own experience and relief at learning, just a few minutes before our session, that her son was safe. I found this out only later, of course. In the moment she was deeply attentive, I suspect using the vehicle of her own earlier distress to tune in and empathise with me. Had she still been worried about her son, I imagine her anxiety levels would have been so stratospherically high she might not have even been able to work at all.

The safety of rigidity

As so many of the therapists I spoke to pointed out, life events which may open them up to their patients' experiences sometimes also cause them to close down, to shut off their ability to empathise in order to spare themselves personal pain. Sometimes it is early trauma which has led someone to train as a therapist, and sometimes trauma visits in the current life of a therapist, through illness, bereavement or loss of income when a service shuts down. Like anyone dealing with trauma, there may be an unconscious effort to avoid revisiting feelings or circumstances which might evoke that earlier, or current trauma. This can lead to an avoidance of issues with clients and to a rigidity of thinking or behaviour to keep the anxiety/fear at bay. Referring particularly to stress and burnout among psychologists, Maslach (1986) points out:

> At the cognitive level there is a narrowing of attentional focus and a greater reliance on stereotyped and rigid thinking. This process interferes with memory, problem solving and decision making and can disrupt complex behaviours. At the emotional level, the major reactions are anxiety, depression, frustration, anger and irritability. These feelings may get repressed in a number of dysfunctional behaviours, such as excessive use of drugs and alcohol, eating disorders, aggression and even suicide. (p. 57)

So, quite naturally, our response to anxiety is not confined to the therapy room, but it may be impossible to keep it *out* of the room. Any of the mechanisms we may use to self-soothe, those that are ultimately harmful, will also have consequences: hangovers, sleepless nights, and irritability are only a few.

There is also an anxious 'intolerance' that can erupt when facing in our clients an inability, or an unwillingness, to 'cope' as we have coped at one or another period of our lives. An experienced integrative therapist, Winifred pointed out how she sometimes struggles with impatience while working with clients she perceives through the viewfinder of her own history. She was forced as a child to fend for herself and sometimes she's tempted to tell her clients to just 'buck up':

> there's a little bit of me still, and I had to really look at this and be self-aware which says, actually I got on with it, just get on with it … for goodness sake, get on with it, so there's a bit of lack of … real lack of empathy there, but hopefully I'm able to stand back from that when I'm working with people.

Winifred isn't alone. I know when clients present with a sense of helplessness in middle age, feeling that change is impossible, my anxiety builds to the point where I want to shout out my own experience. 'For heaven's sake', I want to say to them, 'You're only 40 … or 50 … [or whatever age they are], you aren't dead yet!' This may be a projection of their own intolerance with their position, but there's no doubt that it is also burnt into my psychological template. I have to pull on my internal reins, reminding myself that their history isn't mine, with particularly strong role models who showed me that anything is possible in the middle and later stages of life.

Professional tensions

While Winifred was speaking of her very ability to 'cope' as an interfering element in her work, all but a few of the therapists I spoke to suggested that current anxieties sometimes distracted them from their work. Mark struggled through a period of intense worry when his department was faced with closure. He found the experience extremely distressing, particularly in relation to his clinical work.

> I think, with hindsight, I probably became quite depressed. My sleep and appetite was disturbed and then the service didn't look after us at all, so I think that invariably impacted on my clinical work. I can't think it didn't. I was probably not as engaged with the clients. I think

I was distracted, you know, I mean you're going into these clinical rooms that you've been using for years, and you're aware that you're going to be kicked out of here.

Mark's experience is no different from any other employee facing the prospect of redundancy, and why should it be? Working as a therapist in a busy health clinic may be his 'calling' as many therapists claim, but it is also his occupation, the means by which he pays his bills. As a therapist there is also an emotional attachment we develop with many of our clients and patients. Freudenburger (1986) points out that:

> Professionals who work in institutional settings learn early that they may have virtually no control over the political process that may have impact on their lives and work ... A feeling that one's job is not permanent may additionally lead to anxiety, stress and burnout. (p. 140)

It isn't just the possibility of losing a job that may evoke anxiety within a health service setting. There are increasing pressures on staff to 'perform', to 'get results' and to 'measure' and 'monitor' their patients for signs of 'improvement'. All this in an era of financial cutbacks, a welter of bureaucratic form filling and a weeding out of those people approaching the service who might not fit the 'assessment criteria'. Rizq (2012) argues in her consideration of the British National Health Service's provision of psychological services, that 'a service's repudiation of its explicit anxiety-containing function and its subsequent inability to acknowledge and thoughtfully engage with the suffering, fragility and dependence of patients in its care, results in both conscious and unconscious feelings of loss, anger, grief and guilt within its clinicians, its managers and its patients' (p. 324). In other words, when a therapist is forced to make decisions according to a predetermined and specific set of organised criteria, the exclusionary elements and rigidity of the process 'are likely to create deep and far-reaching anxieties, in both staff and public alike' (Rizq, 2012, p. 325).

Among the therapists I formally interviewed for my study, the only therapists to express disenchantment were those working within institutional settings, feeling the pressure to 'deliver results'. Even the fundamentals of 'containment' sometimes appeared absent, such as the use of the same room each week, or the opportunity to make the choice when ending therapy might be appropriate. As Marshall pointed out:

> When I became a therapist, there's things that happen now that just wouldn't happen then, things like the environment, the change of room, trying to get the same room and, you know, some of the basic

principles have sort of been eaten away, so I do feel like the standard of what we are delivering is not as good as it was 10 years ago. In some ways it probably is, in terms of the way it's monitored and evaluated and audited, but in other ways I think standards have declined. I can understand why it's changing, and I can understand the pressure for numbers and contacts and things like this – I do understand that – but I still think that in order to help people with their mental health problems, we have to protect our mental health. I think some of the pressures that we're working in now probably isn't gonna help us in the long term.

If powerlessness is a precursor for trauma, it stands to reason that it will, at the very least, evoke anxiety, perhaps even contributing to a higher risk of heart disease (Boseley, 2012; Kivimäki *et al.*, 2012). As I have already pointed out, stress does have physical ramifications and, as Gawande writes, all pain is 'in the head' (2003, p. 125). Both pain and anxiety have trigger points within the brain which translate physically, for instance in panic attacks and back pain. Though he is considering the plight of physicians rather than psychotherapists, it isn't difficult to see some parallels:

> Studies point to such 'inorganic' factors as loneliness, involvement in litigation, receipt of workers' compensation, and job dissatisfaction. Consider, for example, the epidemic of back pain in the medical profession itself. Disability insurers once saw doctors as ideal customers. Nothing stopped doctors from working – not years of stooping over operating tables, not arthritis, not even old age … In the last few years however, the number of doctors with disabling back or neck pain has risen dramatically. Needless to say, doctors aren't suddenly being required to carry heavy packages around. But one known risk factor has been identified: with the growing role of managed care, job satisfaction in the medical profession has plunged.
>
> (Gawande, 2003, pp. 119–120)

The pressure to conform

Psychotherapists come in all forms of training modalities, like bags of Liquorice Allsorts. Even within the major traditions – humanistic, for instance – a therapist might be 'gestalt' or 'person-centred'. Someone trained as an integrative psychotherapist may place himself within an 'existential' framework, or, as in my case, a psychoanalytic perspective. However, within institutional health services there is often a prevailing view determining what works and what does not, whether it is psychoanalytical, or cognitive/behavioural. Like the length of hems, modalities can go in and out of fashion. For those therapists who are trained in approaches other than those currently in vogue, the pressure to conform can be considerable, some therapists admitting they chose to do further training in EMDR,[1] or systems therapy, for instance, in order to feel confident or be 'taken seriously' by their bosses and colleagues. Further professional development is essential, of course, but such strategic studying may be at the expense of deeper learning where a therapist can combine personal skills and interests in the better service of her patients and clients.

The pressure to learn something which expressly works against your 'talents' will likely crank up the anxiety levels, like forcing someone who loves to paint abstract pictures into becoming an accountant. You may end up with the piece of paper to say you've done the training, but it doesn't mean you'll use, or retain the learning, or value it very highly (Stobart, 2008). And if you do, you could be miserable, with no one benefiting very much at all, including your patients. As a supervisor of therapists working in primary care within the UK's National Health Service, I can vouch for the level of anxiety that is ratcheted up another notch with every new 'directive' and the encouragement to engage in another form of training, sometimes in tandem and seemingly at odds with one another, for instance 'CBT with Personality Disorders', while having to provide taped material proving they are working effectively with depression within the person-centred approach. These are dedicated professionals, not newbies on the block. Sometimes their despair at the demands placed upon them is tangible, most of the session focusing on the pressures they feel they are under rather than on the patients themselves. This may be appropriate, of course, but there are moments when I wonder at the balance ...

The alternative may simply be to quit the profession, or rise up into administration to avoid working at the coal face with clients and the pressure of providing positive 'data' for those endless studies on therapy effectiveness, and all within a limited number of weeks with very disturbed patients. One of my colleagues finally ended her career after years as a therapist within a health service because she could no longer face the pressure, her anxiety levels rising beyond anything she could cope with. Early retirement seemed to her the only option. 'I just couldn't take it anymore,' she said, 'And the saddest thing is, it was so dreadful and I felt so awful by the time I left, I don't even miss it now.'

Private practice

Those therapists in private practice may not be bound by the strictures of a public health service, but the mechanics and demands of working outside the 'containment' or structure of such a setting may also present additional anxieties. In their seminal paper on 'The Hazards of Being a Therapist', Freudenburger and Robbins (1979) point out that anxiety concerning social status, professional competition, and academic achievement all work towards undermining a therapist, often causing him to grow stale within the therapy room. Patients here, too, become part of a numbers game, each one representing additional income in a life increasingly measured by financial and social success. Again, this leads to a rigid position, a lack of creativity and in their view, a curious twist:

> in time an ironic paradox emerges. Many of the patients seem to live more fully than the therapist. True, the patients were either crazy, impulse-ridden, or talking of feeling empty, dead and depressed. Yet, as their therapy moves along they seem to be more a part of life than the therapist. The therapist's controlled, objective, professional stance seems to mould all his relationships. Trained to listen in order to hear appropriately, the therapist becomes trapped into the position of listening to the sounds of others. Ironically, he may be listening too intensely to be able to hear or follow his own personal drumbeat. Somewhere along this busy path of professionalism, a personal self tends to become lost. (p. 140)

Conclusion

Archaic and current anxieties, the pressure to succeed, to advance or even just hold onto our positions, can all cause us extreme worry and stress, to say nothing of burnout when we work long hours while attempting to keep our family and personal relationships alive. In all of this, we may also long for some time on our own, where no one demands anything of us. Ironically, the office is often our refuge, where we can celebrate, albeit quietly, our achievements with our clients, where we feel good and noble about ourselves, deluding ourselves that we are leaving our anxieties out of the room. Again, paradoxically, we may not be. In order to feel this good at work we may be avoiding issues of anger and hate in our clients, their suggestions that nothing is being accomplished in therapy or that we are inattentive. We may steer clients down more comfortable lines of thought and discussion in order to avoid additional discomfort in ourselves.

Amongst the therapists I spoke to, the more deeply acknowledged the intensity of the experience, the more likely therapists were to admit that it both inhibited and helped in their work with clients and patients. Experience may draw us closer to our clients, but anxiety pries us apart, as Jessica illustrated, our physiological responses to stress sometimes making real contact impossible. This raises a difficult question of how much should we work, if at all, when facing high levels of tension, and when and for how long should we take breaks? As well, how would this even be possible, in a world where clinical work may be our 'vocation', but it is also our livelihood?

Psychotherapists working within mental health settings, as well as those in private practice, face both professional and personal anxieties. No one is spared. There may also be a wish to escape into our clinical work when anxiety is the product of home, rather than a refuge from it. Work as a refuge is a theme we repeatedly return to. As one therapist said to me, 'There was nowhere else for me to go where I could forget.'

Note

1   Eye Movement Desensitisation and Reprocessing.

6 History: a lens to the future

Why we become therapists

> Most therapists possess a high degree of emotional investment in tending to the needs of others. Consequently, it can be narcissistically wounding to discover and to acknowledge the various ways in which their therapeutic efforts serve their own needs and hidden agendas. Not only does such inquiry raise doubts about the meaning and purpose of one's professional activity; it challenges core aspects of one's very personality and worldview.
>
> (Sussman, 2007, p. 192)

While working with a group of actors focusing on trauma, I suggested that all of the characters they were playing – RAF pilots badly burned during bombing raids in World War II (Watkins, 2012) – were likely attracted to such dangerous missions as a result of unconscious motivations, probably located in their histories. How they responded to their current trauma might also be a result of how they had coped in the past. What was their back-story, I inquired? One of the actors piped up and asked me why I had become a therapist. A little surprised by the question, I told them what I have told admission and examining panels for over twenty years. I previously worked as a producer in news and current affairs for the BBC. I knew journalists who were deeply affected by their experiences working in war zones and this had acted as a catalyst to my beginning training, initially as a counsellor.

A few hours later I was still mulling over my response, considering further the difference between the *reason* for my training and the *catalyst* which prompted the move from a successful life in broadcasting to an apparently diverse career as a psychotherapist. Therapists, I believe, are created, not so much in the womb as through their early experiences, either suffering themselves or making brave attempts to alleviate the anguish of those they love. This is also true in my case; my motivation for training might reasonably be reduced to a wish to ameliorate the 'depression' of those around me such as my colleagues in distress after witnessing conflict and profound human despair, and which to some degree replicated my mother's agony following the death of her child when I was less than two years old. The struggle, in my view, rests in the impossibility of the task. There is no cure for or rescue from such suffering, only sometimes recognition and understanding. As a child I wanted my mother to be 'well' in order that she might enjoy me. I wonder how often with clients I have wanted to relieve them of their pain in order that *I* might feel better?

This chapter is concerned with how a therapist's past might help, or hinder, their work with clients. If within us all there is a 'compulsion' to repeat, we may need to guard against our futile, and often unconscious, attempts to remedy the past through our work with clients. On the other hand, while we cannot change the past, there can be transformation in the 'here and now' through recognising the limitations of our control over previous events. Our histories, in fact, for all the training we have undergone, the money we have spent in educating ourselves and the time we have spent hitting the books, may be our greatest resource as therapists. We must not squander it, not just for our own benefit, but in the service of our clients and patients.

Motivation

> You can't avoid the understanding that somehow what attracts us to this sort of work is something to do with our own psychology, our own sort of personality, you know, that we need something to be in that position … I was a parenting child, yes, my mother needed care as it were, not my father, but I was definitely a parenting child. It's a sort of way of life really, and I think I just professionalised it.
>
> (Anna, psychoanalytic)

The motivations behind why therapists become therapists, the 'impossible' profession (along with education and politics!) (Freud, 1937) has been considered most notably by Sussman, who points out that, considering the emphasis placed on understanding our own 'unconscious motivations' during training, it is surprising how little has been written on the subject (2007, p. 2). It is through recognition and understanding of our very complexity, he argues, that we can best reach out to our patients.

> Those who choose to enter the profession typically manifest significant psychopathology of their own, which, if sufficiently understood and mastered, may actually enhance their ability to understand and help their clients. From this perspective, personal suffering is a prerequisite

for the development of the empathy and compassion that characterize competent therapists.

(Sussman, 2007, p. 25)

The argument here is for sufficient self-knowledge, typically acquired at least to some degree, through therapy and deep self-reflection. Bager-Charleson, in her book on 'reflective practice' writes of the '*transformative learning*' that comes from considering her history in relation to her clients.

> Chaos and excessive reflection come as a pair, in my world, incompatible yet inseparable … I have 'recycled' problems, experiences, and what could be called a 'pathology', or, at least, certainly 'wounds', into something potentially useful. (2010, p. 70)

Here, then is the nub of it all: it is not so much that we have struggled at times in our lives, usually early in our history, but how we transform that archaic trauma and distress into something meaningful for ourselves through working as therapists. We need our clients as much as they need us, though our longing may be less explicit. Like Rogers and his admission that working with clients provided him with an intimacy he sometimes found difficult in his personal life (1990, p. 47), we are all looking for something transformative in our work with patients. The danger of course is when we 'enact' unresolved trauma from our past (Mann and Cunningham, 2008), at one end of the spectrum perhaps avoiding or seeking out something of our own experience in our client, at the other extreme failing to hold the ethical boundary, gratifying our narcissistic wishes through abusing those who come to us for help.

The majority of therapists, I believe, function from a position of integrity, consciously working in the service of their clients. Every decent psychotherapy training course emphasises the need for self-awareness, and most programmes now demand at least some experience of personal therapy. However, if the trainee attends therapy only for the sake of collecting the prerequisite hours, true self-awareness, that 'walking through fire' experience of really 'using' therapy and 'working through' personal issues that are often very painful, can easily be avoided. I have heard many experienced therapists express exasperation with trainees they feel are simply 'doing the time'. As I mentioned in Chapter 2, a close colleague, David Mann, has suggested that 'real' therapy only begins with therapists once their training is completed and attendance is by choice, rather than sufferance. However, how many qualified psychotherapists continue therapy beyond the required hours? On the basis of my study, I would suggest they are in the minority, some of them returning only at times of deep crisis. If we are unable to face our pasts, how then can we expect our clients to revisit theirs? As Anthony Storr (1990) also suggests, our histories are fundamental to our training as therapists:

> Psychotherapists often have some personal knowledge of what it is like to feel insulted and injured, a kind of knowledge which they might rather be without, but which actually extends the range of their compassion. (p. 177)

How unfortunate, then, if we are not willing to uncover as much as possible the key to our own histories, even while working towards opening the door to our clients' lives? And issues do not always lie dormant once uncovered in therapy. As Alice expressed in Chapter 2, she was forced to face her primary loss, her longing for children, over and over again at every stage of her life.

Histories: loss and redemption

During my interviews with therapists I repeatedly heard stories of childhood grief, neglect, personal loss and the struggle to care for others. This shouldn't come as a surprise, of course, though frequently I heard variations on the statement, 'I've never really thought about this before,' a surprising remark considering that the majority of therapists in the formal part of my study had undergone therapy at least through the duration of their training. Only two therapists had no experience of counselling or therapy at all, both of them CBT.

Across the board, they linked their choice to become therapists with childhood distress, sometimes an event, as in a sibling's psychotic breakdown, or due to 'cumulative trauma' (Khan, 1964) where neglect or violence, for instance, were generally threatened or exerted. For many therapists, the demands imposed on them as children became a way of life and, in Anna's words, they simply 'professionalised' their early experience by becoming psychotherapists. Many reported some form of abandonment during their childhood, through alcohol, bereavement, divorce or in the case of three therapists, the death of a parent which resulted in also being sent to boarding school. Being sent away to school was invariably reported as traumatic, although the intention had been 'for their own good'. As Duffell reports (2000), this is the prevailing reason parents send their children away, though it invariably results in trauma, a profound rupture to the attachment between mother and child often leading to relationship difficulties in adult life. How much more severe might that trauma be if the child is sent away following the death of a parent, in each of the cases in my research study, the death of the father? Seven therapists reported experiencing violence as children, including sexual abuse.

Choice of model in which to train

All but four of the therapists in this study directly related their choice to become a therapist to their early history, and all but one of those could link their history directly to the *kind* of therapist they became. In the instance of the sole therapist who did not relate her choice of model to her history, Taylor said that she had been given the opportunity to study CBT within the health system and she did not want to turn it down. She had been a 'wild child', out of control and headed for prison when an early marriage and children forced her to 'settle down' and consider her future as a single mother. She did not want to repeat her parents' mistakes, where violence and neglect were the main features, and so she went to work at a hospital nearby, initially as a nurse's helper before studying to become a nurse. In her late thirties she was offered the opportunity to train as a therapist. When Taylor began her training, she was enthusiastic about the possibility of tangible outcomes.

> I had an interest in psychotherapy full stop, but I think I was more interested in something that worked, something that you could offer to people with problems ... It [CBT] was something that was observable, measureable; you were giving things to people that they could take away and use for evermore.

As she developed as a practitioner, Taylor also became more aware of other models of therapy, admitting that a humanistic model would be more suited to her approach to life now. Congruence, empathy and unconditional positive regard (Rogers, 1957) underlie much of how she relates to her clients. But while she is drawn to the Rogerian approach, she also clearly values the notion of 'results', appreciating the pragmatic focus of the cognitive/behavioural tradition. While ostensibly a CBT therapist, she clearly works from her own, integrated model which suits who she is and how she perceives life.

Mark is another therapist who directly links his choice to train as a CBT practitioner to events in his childhood. His father tragically and unexpectedly died when he was young and his early experiences dealing with his mother's grief had a profound impact on his choice to become a therapist.

> I remember once watching my mother – I can remember it clearly as though it was yesterday – on a Saturday, absolutely distraught in tears. She was cleaning in the kitchen and I'm observing this as the – I

don't know how old I was, I might have been nine or 10 or something, wanting to fix this pain that she's experiencing. I can't do it, it's like what do you do with this? And I mean, I remember now, because I used to do a paper round at that time, I was well below my age, I shouldn't have been doing it, and I went out and I bought her a new tea towel. That was my way of trying to kind of help but realising, actually, it doesn't help.

Mark links his decision to train as a CBT therapist to those early experiences of helplessness in the face of his mother's grief and despair. He believes that his attraction to a tradition which is 'evidenced based' is no accident. He wanted to help his mother, to 'fix' her grief.

I think all therapists go to whatever they do because it works where they're coming from, and for me, it [CBT] works for my personality. The evidence-based [model] just feels more genuine with the clients ... I remember when I got to where I got to, having been through all these different things, it just felt right. I thought, yeah, this is where I'm meant to be.

As a CBT therapist, Mark uses 'tools'. He is able to impart ways of managing to his clients and to revise their 'negative thinking' (Greenberger and Padesky, 1995). Within his work he is able to feel that he provides for his clients in a way, perhaps, that he could not with his mother. Mark may be unconsciously replaying the moving account of his own attempt to alleviate his mother's despair with the gift of a tea towel, this time with clients and, in his mind, to more effect. Perhaps each client represents his boyhood, grieving mother.

Therapy: an attempt to master the past?

One of the signposts of trauma is a feeling of 'powerlessness', the merciless truth that there is 'nothing' we can do to change events. Finding a sense of 'meaning' may help, enabling a sense of mastery over current events or making plans for the future, but it will never cancel out the original trauma, a corner of ourselves forever transformed.

Malcolm was in his early teens when his older brother had a psychotic breakdown. He specialises in working with adolescents and systemically, with families. He also has a particular interest in trauma.

My brother was ill on and off for ... I mean he still is ill, but he was ill on and off for a long time, and I moved into adolescence and he was this kind of ill person that was taking away all the attention that I felt that I needed. It was a very difficult time, and I was very angry at him for being unwell and I didn't understand it at all. He was quite actively psychotic and doing very, very strange things all the time. I remember that he would play his music half speed, or be in the yard talking to Martians ... and it really made me think about it and I think, as I got older, I realised that what he had was actually a mental illness and he wasn't doing it just to annoy me ...

Malcolm, interestingly, avoids working with psychosis, focusing instead on children who were the same age he was at the onset of his brother's illness, during the period he found so difficult during his own adolescence. After studying psychology in university, Malcolm trained specifically in CBT, pointing out that:

It's very active and you can sort of give the client stuff to do and to make them feel better about themselves and I quite like that it's quite an active therapy. It's very opposite to my experience of my brother where I was very inactive and couldn't do anything and felt very helpless and kind of powerless.

Malcolm and Mark both felt the need to relieve their sense of powerlessness over their circumstances, to find a way to manage their personal crisis. When I suggested to Malcolm that his interest in adolescents might stem from his own experience as a teenager living with a mentally ill brother he said:

Oh dear. It's funny isn't it. You kind of do these things but you don't always think about them in that way. I suppose you spend so much time thinking about other people, as a therapist, that you spend a lot less time thinking about you, you don't have time to think about yourself, it just doesn't happen so much.

The need for something concrete, for something more tangible and evidenced based is clearly important for those therapists training in branches of the cognitive/behavioural tradition. They are less the philosophers of the therapy world than they are the craftsmen, with something physical resulting from all their hard work. Where the challenge may arise is in the 'failure' of their efforts to help particular clients. Malcolm admits that the adolescents he sees are 'siphoned' off into other services if they show symptoms of psychosis. However, evidence of change in the kids he works with is important to his self-confidence as a therapist:

What I notice about myself is that if I'm with a particular client for a long time, and there isn't a huge amount of change, I have to be careful that I don't start thinking to myself, oh, I'm not very good, you're a bad therapist because you haven't managed to do something with this person, and I'm aware that I have a kind of insecurity about that, so I'm kind of learning over the years I suppose to step back a bit more and to actually sort of look at it from a different perspective.

We all need success as therapists – where would the job satisfaction be otherwise – but we may need to guard against either not working with those who do not meet our requisite for 'positive results', or encouraging those clients who are 'eager to please' from re-enacting aspects of their early trauma. Part of what our clients need from us is an ability to live and survive our own disappointment and to accept what 'we cannot change'.[1] CBT therapists, as well as many humanistic practitioners, do not actively work with the transference, but there must be some recognition that elements of personal and archaic trauma will play out in every relationship, and inevitably within the therapy room. 'This will start off about me,' said one client to me many years ago, 'but it will end up about you.' Over and over again in our sessions we returned to her tendency to forfeit her own experience to spare me the discomfort of mine. This perceptive young woman simply articulated a truth that plays out in a multitude of therapeutic relationships in every tradition: it starts off all about them, but we need to beware that it doesn't end up all about us.

Case study: managing the unmanageable

Katy also had to deal with psychosis in the family as a child. Her father was schizophrenic and her mother, she says, would now be diagnosed as 'borderline personality disorder'. Katy's father had 'florid' episodes throughout her childhood and which continue to this day when he refuses to take his medication. For Katy, there has been some relief from the pressure and trauma of her early years through understanding and finding a way externally to symbolise what was happening to her internally. Katy is an integrative psychotherapist with a particular focus on constellation and gestalt work. She is also trained as an art therapist.

My mother was a cellist and I played the violin and certainly in my childhood that was my refuge always, that I would go off somewhere and play my violin, and that would soothe me … This is why the artistic is so crucial for me. Somehow I found my way to music and expression because I knew I couldn't speak of any of this [father's illness] as a child, and the other thing that I recognise that I did I think, as a young child, was to – and of course I didn't do this consciously, and my family would always joke about how I have my special little box and it would change over the years. And what I've come to see is that, you know, that was something in my external physical reality that showed me what I had done internally, that actually somehow I had placed what was most precious in my box. It meant for a fairly lonely childhood but, yeah, it kept those very precious parts of me safe.

While Malcolm avoids working with psychosis, Katy is comfortable with psychotically disturbed patients, though in her personal life she has put boundaries around her father, no longer 'sorting things' out for him when her father breaks down after neglecting to take his medication. She believes this has strengthened her own ability to remain with her clients, available to them within the therapy room, but not at their mercy, and to ensure that her own current good health continues. This is very different from her early years as a therapist when she felt obliged to manage one of her father's breakdowns and to respond to his constant demands for attention.

It coincided with a time in my practice when I was probably working with one, two, three clients who … two who had been given a diagnosis of dissociative identity disorder and one who was very schizoid … It was a tremendously challenging period to have this in my working life, and then to know that no sooner would I have kind of gone out for my run and start making my supper and having a conversation with my partner, that you know either my brother or my father would be on the phone.

Katy recognised she had to 'walk my talk' and ensure she had a group of people around her who would 'hold' her patients at times of crisis, in case she needed to leave suddenly. She also had to ensure that she had personal support.

One of the first things I did was to let my therapist at that time know, my body psychotherapist, this is what's going on for me, what do we do if I need extra sessions, is that an option, and talking through with her, you know, I really need to lay out for myself and to see for myself. And because I'm very visual I needed to literally, physically lay it out with her – who is there in my life who's going support me with this 'cause I don't want to go crazy.

Making use of therapy and supervision, relying on colleagues to support her is essential to Katy's well-being as a therapist. As Secunda (1997) asserts in *When Madness Comes Home*, those who suffer with mental health issues also need to take responsibility for managing their illness, including taking their medication. Over the years Katy has learned to pull back from the impossible demands of family pressures and now, she says, she would do things very differently if her father collapsed.

> Now, I would give less time to the family ... I think there was a part of me that didn't have the strength at the time within myself, psychically or in any way to say, you know Dad we can put these things in place for you. I know you're probably gonna dismantle them all, so what do we do, do we put them in place, or do we not bother? I did my usual [then], got into parentified child and, okay, do all these things, so I know for sure now I wouldn't do that ... I would have one conversation with the GP and say this is what I can offer, this is what I can't offer, this is what I'm not gonna do, and I think it was also very hard to do that at the time. Most of it of course was my process, within myself, but I think it was also the entanglements that I had with my brother at that time too, in terms of if I don't do this, it's all gonna fall on Barry, and if it all falls on Barry, he's gonna collapse, and I don't wanna see my brother go crazy.

Katy struggles with not just her past, but the 'living' repetition of her childhood in the present where the themes of dependence and rejection continue, as does the constant fear that either she, or her brother, may collapse into psychosis. Katy is able, in her own words, to work with 'themes of craziness', her history giving her a particular understanding and 'feel' for her clients. Is Katy, in her work with such damaged or ill patients, managing to provide help in a way that she was, and still is, unable to provide for her father? When asked what client group she might avoid working with, Katy was very clear that she now refuses to work with clients who do not want to 'let go' of their story and who will take years of 'going round' before there is even a little bit of a 'breakthrough'. For those clients, she says, there are therapists who will be far more patient. In other words, perhaps Katy does not want to work with those clients who, like her father, reject what she has to offer by 'dismantling' any help she might be able to provide.

The power of relationship

If CBT therapists are the 'fixers' of the business, psychoanalytic psychotherapists may reasonably be seen as their polar opposites, who need to 'understand' in order to manage their difficulties. 'Fixing', in their view, is not possible, but reaching an understanding of how events played out and *why* they did, is fundamental to engaging in meaningful and healthier relationships in the 'here and now'.

Case study: coming alive

Raymond is a psychoanalytic therapist who suffered abuse as a child, both physically and mentally. Born in Canada, his father was a British serviceman sent for military training to Alberta in the middle of the war. For years he believed that someone else was his father. His mother was neglectful and cruel, often referring to him inexplicably as the 'bastard' until his mid-teens when he finally learned the truth.

Raymond's isolation, both physically and emotionally, was so complete that by the time he attended school he still could not speak. His older brother, he says, had to translate his 'gabble' for him. Raymond believes that his focus on the 'relational' in his work and his belief in the power of 'attachment' theory (Bowlby, 1991) is rooted in his history.

> I just found that other approaches weren't really helpful in the world as much as attachment theory. The type of therapist I am, I suppose, I'm very relational in that it's very participatory. I'm not a blank screen. I want to reach someone. I think that, again, might well be to do with my personal history of being quite dissociated and not reached.

Raymond left school in his mid-teens, escaping first of all into a low-paying job washing dishes in a hamburger joint. He discovered he liked cooking, moving from restaurant to restaurant and gradually learning the skills of a master chef. Eventually he ran his own kitchen. He also recognised that what had kept him safe as a child, the ability to gauge other people's moods, stood him in very good stead as a chef.

> I used that skill to keep my kitchen staff happy. There was a lot of pastoral care, bereavements, quite a bit of marital problems. You're the first port of call as the boss, so any theft, drink or drug problems, you know, I had to deal with.

Finally, Raymond decided he also wanted to change his profession and to work more closely with people. He trained initially as a psychodynamic counsellor, and later as a psychotherapist. With his own history of delayed development, Raymond has an appreciation for those people who have also suffered childhood trauma.

One of the things I've found with a lot of people who come, they say 'I think I've got Asperger's' or 'I'm a bit autistic', and more often than not it's a similar sort of background that I had where they really haven't had attuned care giving. In Winnicottean terms, the childhood spontaneous gesture just has not been greeted.[2] They've had to develop a false self but also become emotionally detached and rather dissociated from their own affective life. They're a bit dead emotionally, a lot of people.

It was Winnicott who said, 'it is a joy to remain hidden, but a disaster not to be found' (1963, p. 186). For Raymond, it is the very lack of attunement in his own childhood which allows him to tune in so powerfully to those clients who suffer such isolation and emotional detachment from others. They are brought to 'life', sometimes for the first time, through Raymond's ability to cut through that deadness and create a spark of recognition. Raymond provides hope, if you like, through understanding, recognition of his own developmental deficits providing him with a powerful tool within his therapeutic relationships.

If we often, as therapists, find a route back to ourselves through therapy, either receiving or providing it, a kind of emotional rapprochement can also be achieved in the course of our personal lives, engaging in meaningful relationships and developing positive role models. Becoming a parent, too, as I discuss in Chapter 2, can have a profound effect on our development as therapists. Raymond believes that it was working through the transference in therapy and having children of his own which helped him become emotionally alive. He admits, however, that something of his 'darker side' has never been challenged in therapy.

> It does beg the question whether everything needs to be fully resolved, and to what extent it can be, as long as you're not acting it out with a client, or if the inevitable enactments occur that you're able to have this 'generative split' that Bollas[3] talks about, where there is the experiential ego and the observing ego and so you can become embedded in the client's madness or distress, but there's also the other part of the experiencing side that is observing and … helping you dis-embed and do some repair work.

Raymond is no longer in therapy, but he does have weekly supervision, which he also views as therapeutic. In addition, he engages in peer supervision and has close collegial contacts from whom he receives regular support. He has, in effect, created the kind of supportive 'family' around him he did not have as a child. This 'family' enables him to maintain a 'robustness' which he believes enables him to work even during difficult, personal crises.

It's not quite compartmentalisation, but it is a matter of when you're in a room with the person, something happens where there is that engagement, which enables me at least to leave the rest of it outside the room in a good enough way. I might come into the room looking for something, you know, the client might pick something up, but that can be dealt with, and I feel that I can then give them my attention, engage with them in a relational way, and work with them. I also think that, in a broader way, it probably reflects a lot of the reasons why we become therapists. We get something from our clients. I think Patrick Casement's book, you know, *Learning From The Patient*,[4] not only learning from them, it's also in a very mutual way that we're being healed by them as well as hopefully we're healing them. I think it's very important to understand that process so that we're not actually playing our own needs out with the client and it can get a bit tricky, but I don't think we can leave out of the frame either that we're getting something from the work too, that can be healing. In a vicarious way sometimes it's healing for us to be working with other people's problems.

Raymond is clearly thoughtful and self-reflective, acknowledging there is a darker side to himself never explored in therapy. How, then, does he distinguish between what might be 'healthy' job satisfaction and the more 'perverse' use of a client to simply self-sooth or gratify ourselves?

Yes, there's something going on there, and that raises a question: what are the safeguards, you know, of in a sense not quite abusing the patient, but maybe exploiting or using the patient in a way too much for your own needs, rather than for their needs. There are various ways of thinking about that. One is really ongoing monitoring, close monitoring of your own counter-transference. I'm in weekly supervision, have been ever since I trained and qualified, and I think that's a real safeguard with a trusted senior colleague to be able to talk openly, honestly, about what's going on, and it can be an erotic aspect. I've got a young woman at the moment who, you know, there is that erotic side going on, very strongly, mutually, and you know that needs to be maintained and managed without, again, being acted out, and that both needs addressing in the therapy, but also with a trusted colleague, consultation supervision, so there's the monitoring of the counter-transference.

Raymond has given a lot of thought to his role in the therapeutic relationship, how his own history might affect his work with patients. He sits 'face-to-face' with his clients, rather than using the couch. By his own admission this is also a reflection of his own need to be 'mirrored' in a relationship as well as his firm belief that this is what his patients need, perhaps above all else. As Yalom says: 'It is the relationship that heals' (1980, p. 401). As it is for the patient, so it is also for the therapist.

Fighting dogma: history playing out in the 'here and now'

How we react to events in our lives is largely based on how we have managed events previously. And how we do that is often based on how we learned to deal with struggles in our childhood, taking clues from our carers, sometimes repeating their patterns despite ourselves, so ingrained are our internalised objects (Fairbairn, 1994; Guntrip, 1992; Winnicott, 1963).

Francine is a humanistic practitioner who trained initially as a gestalt therapist. She grew up in an intellectual family; both her parents were socialists who fervently believed in the 'collective' and the corrupting influence of capitalism. They were also teachers and Francine's childhood was spent within an impoverished community in the Canadian North, living among the Aboriginal population where social deprivation was the norm, but belief in the collective was also incorporated into the culture.

> My intellect is a strong resource and choosing Gestalt as my training was fairly deliberate. I realised, having tried some tasters, that actually my intellectual development sort of outpaced my emotional development. My ability to identify and express my feelings needed more attention and Gestalt seemed, certainly in those days, 1970s/80s, was very emotion focused and so that seemed like, okay, this feels like its filling in gaps in my whole education as a person. But I'm aware that, although that was maybe some kind of semi-conscious attempt to counterbalance, I still find, you know, I will reach for concept. I will reach for ideas readily. It's just very much in me as a sort of heritage, family heritage.

There's no getting away from her history, according to Francine, though she works hard to flex her psychological muscles in new ways, training in a form of therapy that emphasises the feeling experience of the here and now, but at moments of crisis and stress she reverts to reliance on her intellect, her default position.

Growing up in a socialist household has also presented some inhibitors to her work: while she works within the Canadian national health system at the moment, she also has a private practice, but it is small and she struggles to let people know she is in 'business'. The sense of social responsibility imbued from childhood 'has made the idea of becoming an entrepreneurial psychotherapist anathema'. She believes her archaic 'guilt' shines through, limiting her ability to successfully develop and run a private practice. On the other hand, she recognises that her resistance to dogma of any sort is also rooted in her unusual upbringing, her parents' political and anti-religious stance so forceful that she learned early on the importance of 'listening' to others.

> I learnt from them a real, almost a kind of allergic reaction to dogma, so I'm very sort of hot, when I'm listening to clients and I'm hearing the 'should' coming out ... I think it's also helped to develop what I believe is an important stance to have as a psychotherapist of 'not knowing' in that I may form some judgement about a person sitting in front of me. I'm very conscious of the impact of pre-judgement and prejudice, really conscious, you know, it filters through from the generations. My parents and grandparents weren't involved in the Holocaust, but it filters through the kind of stories from more distant relatives, so I [believe in] the importance of respecting and listening to the individual.

While Francine's parents were dogmatic about not being dogmatic, other therapists also related stories of claustrophobic childhoods, lives defined by the community and narrow belief systems in which they were raised. Breaking loose was invariably described as difficult, as it meant leaving behind the safety of belief systems in which decisions are easy because they are based on clearly defined structures of right and wrong. Like many of our clients, when moving away from the family 'system', those therapists also risked banishment from the core group, leaving behind those they love most deeply.

Richard, too, has struggled to move away from 'dogma'. Growing up in the southern United States, at the age of sixteen he was an 'elder' within the religious sect his parents adhered to, a way of life that was all-encompassing. The world was viewed from the position of the sect's belief in a charismatic leader and anyone outside the faith was doomed to perdition. In his twenties Richard struggled to break free. He was sent to Britain to 'convert' others. Exposed to new ideas and arguments refuting the sect's position, he began to realise that 'you could rationalise anything'. His determination to unpick those childhood beliefs led him to 'escape', living for a time with his grandparents up north who supported him while he made up for his 'lost' education. He worked during the day and attended high school at night before going on to university to study psychology.

For Richard, it was his need to 'unpick' the dogmatic thinking of his history which led him to train further as a cognitive therapist, his wish to be released from what felt to him like an intellectual stranglehold. He believes this gives him more insight with clients who present with issues of faith, and interestingly, he once had a member of the sect attend his clinic. Confused at first, he ultimately made the decision to self-disclose. 'When you leave the community you leave everything behind; your parents, your friends, everything that is familiar. Even with support like I had, it's very, very difficult, and deeply lonely. I wanted him to know that I understood what he was speaking about, but I was also clear that this was his decision to make and not mine.'

Self-disclosure is always a difficult call, and we can never be actually sure it will be in the service of the client so much as a means of venting our own anxiety. On the other hand, for the client to know that his therapist has such a deep understanding of his predicament may be both soothing and reassuring, enabling him to consider the possibility of another kind of life through witnessing Richard having emerged so successfully the other side of the sect. He may also fear his judgement, or be unduly influenced by his decision to leave. However, through self-disclosure Richard may also be offering his client an opportunity for a clearer thought process, for the 'elephant in the room' laid out between them to be considered openly.

Entrenched positions

Years ago I worked night shifts, a way of life I found both physically and emotionally draining. There were many advantages to the job, not the least of which was a good salary. I knew people would kill to be in my position and so I remained in the job for far too long, despite a prevailing emotional cocktail of sadness and despair only alleviated when I finally began training as a counsellor. Finally, I could see an end in sight.

Years later I worked with a client who worked night shifts. The job was very demanding and both physically and emotionally strenuous, just as mine had been. He often appeared exhausted during his sessions with me and I felt what I believed was a deep empathy for him. I often expressed my concern, encouraging him to consider the purpose and meaning behind what he was doing.

Finally, one day he leaned forward in his seat and looked me dead in the eye. 'Sometimes I think you *want* me to leave my job!' he snapped, 'I *like* my job! I just don't like the hours I'm having to keep at the moment.'

He was absolutely right. I *had* wanted him to leave his job, to do what I had done and find a way out. Except he didn't want one. I was so blinded by my own history of working in a job I actively found unsatisfying for too long, I had not listened to him at all. This client eventually ended his stint on night shifts and moved on into exactly the area of expertise he had been aiming for. I, on the other hand, needed to let go of my perspective and give in to his, to offer him a truer level of empathy.

We all have our particular positions – philosophical, political, and spiritual – to say nothing of our position within the therapeutic tradition in which we practise. How dogmatic are we, even in our defence 'against' dogma? Entrenchment in any belief system and a resistance to the idea that any other might have value is surely a defensive position. Why are we so afraid? Watching someone 'retreat' into a 'closed' system – whether religious, political or a lifestyle choice – is always difficult for those on the outside who believe they have attained freedom through alternative perspectives. As Francine and Richard show, we need to be open to others' choices, and to sit with 'not knowing'. The temptation for Richard to actively encourage his client to leave the sect must have been mighty strong, and for Francine to work with clients who find safety in 'dogma' may be equally difficult. I will always be grateful to my client for having the courage to stand up to me, to challenge my position and force me to consider how, in the *name* of empathy, I had negated his experience altogether.

Case study: tolerating violence

Marcia is a humanistic therapist. Although she runs a private practice from her home, three days a week she works within a large, high-security prison in Western Australia. She comes into contact with murderers, rapists, and violent criminals on an hourly basis.

> I grew up with a violent, alcoholic father and my stepmother was often taking overdoses and slashing her wrists and there'd be blood and all sorts of things in my house, painkillers, sleeping tablets, all sorts of things … it was my last stepmother, but she was with me for my formative years, between five and 13, … and that was where I got the [idea that] there's nothing more despicable and disgusting than somebody who tries to take their life because that was what I grew up with my father and stepmother … I grew up with my thermostat pretty high.

This notion that suicide is 'despicable' means that she sought out therapy as a young adult, rather than resorting to self-annihilation. However, during my interview with her she was clearly taken aback by the connection she made herself between her violent history and her capacity to withstand the projections and counter-transference of violent offenders in her day-to-day work life. Until our interview she also admitted that she had not considered that 'survival' each day after encountering such violence in her clients was a way of playing out childhood scenarios, enlivening the mundane nature of ordinary life with the high-octane pressure of potential violence. I wondered if Marcia had any kind of radar for fear?

An extremely bad one. It takes a lot for me to be afraid and to some degree [I'm] happier, not happier, more comfortable when slightly [afraid] … Actually, to be with drug addicts and prisoners, is my comfort zone … when I'm in a room with really violent self-abuse [it's] like 'bring it on' [someone] who, you know, goes around stabbing people and watches other people. I've had some amazingly violent clients who sort of cut people's faces open from there to there with Stanley knives, and that's okay for me to sit with. That's been okay.

If Marcia finds the threat of violence her 'comfort zone', the opposite is also true. She finds gentleness difficult to tolerate.

It's a huge challenge, because the calm, just comfortable, loving, every day which my partner is very capable of offering, is hugely threatening for me. It's not comfortable, it's like what do I do with this, what do I do with this, and a lot of time I will almost sort of try to provoke an argument. It's a tough one for me.

Marcia's ability to tolerate the potential for violence may aid in her work with prisoners much of the time but, conversely, it might not be helpful in her work when the pace is slower, or quieter; she may unconsciously want to raise the emotional stakes a little higher simply to enliven the contact, to put herself back in her 'comfort zone'.

It's just something I'm constantly having to look at, as to whether it's self-abusive, or whether it's therapy for myself that I'm [seeking out] … it's also a matter of judging, am I of most use if I'm just doing this gratuitously?

Marcia is a person-centred therapist and she recognises that it is 'not of any use to a client' if she is *only* capable of sitting in the room with a violent offender. She also needs to be able 'to sit with that part of myself', to connect with the other in a meaningful and accepting way. Not condoning their actions, but accepting who they are.

The day that I saw that I wasn't normal in a lot of society's [eyes] was very helpful for me, to see that actually to be cutting people was quite … you know it's not okay, it's not okay, and that was – you know it was a hard one for me to sort of sit with, but it's actually a balance which is slowly coming together for me with clients for being able to be with it, but also the knowledge that it's not okay, yeah.

Marcia has worked hard to give meaning to a difficult history, a history which also means she is able to work with a group of clients many therapists would find impossible or even feel an outright aversion towards. However, she also finds it difficult sometimes to sit with kindness, even in her personal life. It is as if she has an intolerance of personal peace, as if life dips intolerably towards boredom if there is too much calm, or intimacy. Through the counter-transference, is she seeking to repair the struggle of her childhood relationships, to find a way through the violence and seek out the human being? Through the effectiveness of her own ability to work within such a difficult context, is she also providing therapy for herself?

Professionalising history

Many of those I spoke to have had to formulate the story of their own lives, finding symbolisation of their suffering through the development of a vocabulary and a structured narrative to give their experience meaning. Often therapy helped them to confront and make sense of histories that were full of deprivation and heartache.

So many of the therapists in my study suffered as children, many of them in extreme circumstances where neglect and cruelty were the order of things, and in some cases through life events, the death of a parent, or mental health. But others suffered more subtly, perhaps, through a parent's incapacity to empathise or tune in to their child, or through life events which could not be avoided. I am increasingly aware that as a result of my history, I often work very hard to 'enliven' others to ensure that they are present for me. The death of my sister was not the product of intentional, or wanton, cruelty, but it has affected the way I live and how I relate to others. Like Raymond, I am not a 'blank screen' therapist, and I also sit facing my patients. But I must also ask myself the question: when, in my own clinical work, do I struggle to sit with the 'deadness' in others? I want, of course, to bring them 'life'. And when I cannot, when my depressed or passive clients cling to the wreckage of their despair and, in my view, resist any attempt to alleviate their suffering, I often feel a failure as a therapist. When do I face my unbearably sad mother all over again within the therapy room? When can I not, in any way at all, save her from her grief?

If we, as therapists, 'professionalise' what we have done in some way all our lives, are we then able to assume that we also need to derive job satisfaction from the very practice that often left us feeling powerless as children? To feel the 'defeat', or the impossibility of solving the difficulties of our history again in our work would likely make life intolerable. It is the very job satisfaction that provides us with meaning, finally being able to achieve with our clients and patients what, possibly, we could not in our childhoods.

However, linking our pasts with our current view of the world may demand that we forfeit our belief in autonomy: after all, if we are so driven by our past that we have unconsciously pursued a career that either repeats or perpetuates the anxieties of our childhood, what is the point of what we do as therapists? Do we really believe we can conquer our pasts, or do we simply believe that we can manage the consequences through a deeper understanding of what drives us? This clearly will have an impact on our clients or patients and may also mean that when we are faced with a client who views the world through a 'management' lens, we are on a hiding to nothing working towards 'insight'. This does not, of course, take into account the client who defends himself against feeling through rationalising, but it may be worth considering at a deeper level that not one method works for everyone, that no single drug will solve all experiences of 'depression' or physical pain.

None of us, as therapists, can work effectively without some emotional texture to our past. As Frankl (1959) points out, every life needs suffering, and in our work as therapists it also means that we are able to make a bridge between others' suffering and our own, creating an empathic connection, one human being to another. Without this 'life experience' we can provide nothing to our patients and clients. So, how do we ensure that we are deriving 'job satisfaction' for ourselves, but also working to the benefit of our patients and clients? When are we exercising therapy for ourselves at the *expense* of our clients, and when are we *enabling* those we work with through our ability, like Marcia, to sit with the unbearable? As she movingly pointed out, it isn't enough just to be able to 'sit' with the other, we need to make some connection with that part of ourselves that may echo in some way that part of them. In analytical terms, we need to survive their projections and transform them into manageable material that our patients can then begin to work with themselves (Casement, 1985; Klein, 1946). This can be a deeply painful experience, for both therapist and patient, a reducing of both to a common human denominator. Therapy, ultimately, is a personal business for the therapist as well as the client, both of us in the muck and turmoil together.

Notes

1 Saint Francis of Assisi.
2 Winnicott, D. W. (1990), *The Maturational Processes and the Facilitating Environment*. London: Karnac.
3 Bollas, C. (1987), *The Shadow of the Object*. London: Free Association Books.
4 Casement, P. (1985), *On Learning From the Patient*. London: Routledge.

7 Keeping our house in order

'Home is where the heart is.' Or at least we hope it is, a sanctuary or a refuge, a place to put our feet up and escape the tensions of the working world. These days, though, the division between work life and personal life is not as differentiated as it once was, and it isn't just therapists who work from home. We live in a global village where the concept of a home/office is not unusual, and sometimes both partners are in residence all day long, absorbed in entirely different professional disciplines. This is certainly true in my case. However, as already mentioned in Chapter 2, therapists working from home can make things particularly awkward for other members of the family. Young children are forced to play 'quietly' so as not to disturb the patients and often activities need to be curtailed during hours of business – no cooking smells for instance, or noisy household appliances. Even in my household, these days consisting of only the two of us, I have wanted to cringe at the sound of my husband's muffled voice on the telephone leaking through the floor boards, or on one memorable occasion, a cheerful bellow, 'I'm home!' bursting through from the front door when he wasn't aware I was seeing a client.

When a therapist works from home, all spontaneity must cease during clinical hours, unless you are lucky enough to have a separate office space with industrial-strength sound proofing. Family members are forced to tip-toe around, erasing any evidence of their existence while mummy/daddy/partner spends quality time with strangers.

But office space is expensive, regardless of where we live, and may even be prohibitive for many therapists in private practice. We might also overwork at times in order to pay for such accommodation, setting up a dreadful cycle of pressure where we need our clients to remain in therapy in order for us to pay the rent. During times of crisis we possibly take even less time out due to the additional financial demands of paying for an office. Our kids could be happily shouting the house down at home, and our partners slamming around the kitchen with pots and pans, but we are desperately scrabbling to find enough clients who will stay long enough that we can pay the bills.

Money talks

Therapists have a complicated relationship with money, regardless of the tradition in which they work. In a profession largely comprised of people wanting to support others, the fact that money enters into the equation at all can sometimes feel 'dirty', an interference with the more 'noble', or presumed altruistic aspects of psychotherapy. Are we in the business of 'selling' what actually should come for 'free'? Anyone in private practice has undoubtedly heard a client bemoan the fact that he is now 'paying' for what should have been his in the first place; deep attunement to his early suffering, love without conditions, and respectful boundaries. And he is right, they should have been provided as a matter of course. So how do we equate our need to make a living with the fact that much of what we provide should be available without charge?

Most of us train for many years, our (expensive) professional development continuing throughout our careers. Regardless, many of us blanche at openly discussing money, perhaps fearing that our value will be measured, as we may in turn measure others, by the size of our fees. As Kottler (2010) points out:

> We can't agree on whether therapy takes a short time or a long time, whether it ought to focus on the past or the present, whether the therapist or the client should define the problem we are to work on, or even whether the therapist should talk a lot or a little. And perhaps more important, we cannot decide whether therapy is essentially a profession or a business. (p. 120)

Freud (1913) believed that paying for treatment increased a patient's respect for the therapist and this, in turn, diminished some of his or her resistance to therapy. Even in those early days of psychoanalysis, Freud points out that regardless of the length and expense of the training psychoanalysts undertake, they are never likely to earn as much as physicians. Regardless, a therapist must place some value on herself. The financial transaction between client and therapist is vital, Freud argues, indicating a willingness to move further into difficult psychological territory.

> An analyst does not dispute that money is to be regarded in the first instance as a medium for self-preservation and for obtaining power;

but he maintains that, besides this, powerful sexual factors are involved in the value set upon it. He can point out that money matters are treated by civilized people in the same way as sexual matters – with the same inconsistency, prudishness and hypocrisy. The analyst is therefore determined from the first not to fall in with this attitude, but, in his dealings with his patients, to treat money matters with the same matter-of-course frankness to which he wishes to educate them in things relating to sexual life. He shows them that he himself has cast off false shame on these topics, by voluntarily telling the price at which he values his time.

(Freud, 1913, p. 130)

Adjusting to circumstances

Several years ago I left my busy practice in the big city to move to a more rural setting, a beautiful town on the south coast of England. I 'hung up my shingle' as they say in Canada, indicating that I was open for business and waited for clients and patients to roll in.

Except they didn't, or at least only a few pitched up, certainly not enough to define my working life as anything nearing a professional 'practice'. This concerned me as I believe that if we are 'teaching', we should also be practising, not so removed from the clinical experience that we begin to expound from a purely theoretical position, rather than the lived and complex understanding that comes from working with clients.

Moving into town I let people know I was open for referrals. I made contact with a few local therapists and registered on a few websites, paying extra for a top listing. This particularly irked as my last name, starting with 'A', usually means I am at the top of most listings, a lucky happenstance I had for years clearly considered a 'right'. I swallowed my pride and handed over the money. In addition, I also began teaching in a nearby city, a surefire way of making myself more visible.

Still, there were only a trickle of phone calls, a few emails and a couple of inquiries that seemed to dry up at the end of any conversation that involved my fee. 'But I'm worth it,' I wanted to shout, by this time not really convinced myself.

In the big city, my rate had sat pretty much within the middle ground of average. Here in the country, though, I was sky high.

By now you're likely to have figured out at least half of my difficulty. I was resistant to lowering my fee. Having worked so hard over the years to garner professional qualifications, I thought my hourly charge, though high for the neighbourhood, also reflected my experience. But of course, there were other well-qualified therapists in the area, some with greater experience and clearly far more wisdom than I was exercising at the time. Following so many years of small, incremental increases in my previous practice, I found it very difficult to lower my fee. And I'm not talking a little drop here, but what felt like a solid step back five or ten years.

Another element came into play, even after I dropped my charge to a more reasonable level for the region. My location. Like many therapists, I practise from home. I soon realised that the few clients I did have tended not to come from the town itself, but rather they had chosen the anonymity of a therapist outside the vicinity in which they lived. In a rural area this matters: the twitching of net curtains can raise eyebrows and promote wild speculation. It can be hard work sometimes to maintain privacy in a town where there are family and social connections and often fewer degrees of separation than in an urban setting.

So, here I was, charging less and faced with the prospect of renting an office in the closest city to where I live. This was a double financial whammy at a time when I was dealing with more personal expenses than I had considered when moving to the coast, including a mortgage, house repairs and, infuriatingly, a new car. I was earning less and spending more, not an ideal position. Oh, and have I mentioned, I like buying clothes?

Money! Money! Money!

'Money makes the world go round,' so goes the song from the musical *Cabaret*. We are currently several years into a global recession, with both Europe and America struggling to climb out of the financial hole dug so efficiently during the 'boom' years. Here and there, a few 'green shoots' show through, an increase in house sales, a factory opening up or a rise in the monthly sales figures, but on the whole, nothing moves as rapidly as the politicians' mouths. Perhaps by the time you read this good times will be here again, but for how long?

Therapists are not immune from the vagaries of economic boom and bust. During recessions people may not go for therapy, considering it an unnecessary expense. Even if they have the money, they may fear for the future, putting funds aside instead to carry them over a rainy day. For therapists in private practice, this can mean a change in their own financial circumstances. A number of colleagues I know work within mental health institutions because of the security it gives them.

Except it doesn't. Many health services are cutting back or reorganising to accommodate increasing financial constraints or a change in structure. As Mark pointed out in Chapter 4, he was shattered when he was made redundant. Suffering anxiety leading up to the end of his working life within the health service, he then struggled with depression before setting up his own practice and working as a psychological consultant. Ironically, one of his clients is the very institution which had previously let him go.

Recently a colleague of mine was made redundant from the organisation in which she worked as a consultant psychotherapist. Her husband (a psychologist) was also handed a redundancy notice a week later. Shell-shocked, with two children under ten, they picked up sticks and moved to a less expensive city, living in the short term off the funds they had made from selling their house. Working on the basis of yearly contracts, neither of them had received enough severance pay to see them through a few months, let alone the year it might take them to establish themselves either in private practice or in a new organisational environment.

Another colleague has a husband who is a television producer. For a decade he successfully ran his own company but over the past three years he has not had a single commission. This means my friend is now the sole breadwinner in a household with two adolescents, both of whom have a penchant for expensive sports gear.

No one wants to look too greedy in a profession often associated with selflessness, but at the same time there is often a resentment expressed that we are 'unappreciated and underpaid'. As Kottler says, 'no amount of money could fairly compensate us for the aggravation, intensity, emotional turmoil, conflict, and frustration' we sometimes face (2010, p. 123).

There are therapists who charge over the average rate for their services, sometimes by what to the rest of us in the profession seem like huge amounts. Even in times of dire economic straits, there are always people who have money, and are willing to fork out for what they believe, or hope, are exceptionally good services. This may lock into Mair's (1994) argument that much of what is successful in therapy is down to a 'placebo effect', but it may also be that a therapist is particularly skilled in a specific area, couples' counselling for instance, or work with adolescents. I wonder if we sometimes manage our envy of therapists with the chutzpah to set up in expensive clinics, or advertise their clinical expertise in less subtle ways than the rest of us, by denigrating their entrepreneurial spirit and dismissing the possibility that they are effective therapists *because* they charge more than the rest of us, as if making money and ethical practice are somehow an impossible marriage. Are some of us culturally geared towards such an attitude, starting with Bible stories where a rich man is as likely to reach the gates of heaven as a camel is to pass through the eye of a needle? As Klein (1984) points out, envy is a product of living, alive in all of us, and the truth is we need to work, to pay our mortgages, feed our kids, and hopefully make a little extra for luxuries or that rainy day. We might even forfeit the prospect of a glorious afterlife for a bit of the good life now.

Bankers, the gatekeepers of enormous wealth, have gained a particularly bad name, accused of accepting huge bonuses at a time when they are perceived to have fleeced whole nations. Nonetheless, most of us *want*, or need, more money to keep our various domestic ships afloat. Charging less for our therapeutic services may be 'noble', but it doesn't make us good therapists, anymore than charging a higher rate indicates we are 'bad' ones. It does mean, however, that the profile of our patient group will be different. What for one client may be 'peanuts' for another may be a small fortune. But, as Murdin (2012) argues, money talks, pointing out finally that:

> The vast majority of clinicians work with humanity and intelligence in order to make the process useful to their patients. The task is to balance the needs of the therapist to earn a living against the difficulties of the financial vicissitudes of her patients. She can try not to be so draconian that they disappear underground and to manage the money so that the patient is safely and firmly held within a therapeutic frame. (p. 169)

Modern life

In the age of technology, new ways of working are presenting themselves, via computers and social networks. Most therapists I know working in private practice have a web page and advertise themselves on counselling and psychotherapy websites. We have all had to bite the bullet of modernity; otherwise we would sit in an empty office. The internet is the first port of call for most people in search of a therapist. How well we present ourselves, rather than the quality of our work, is often what draws a client in. 'Branding' has become a hot issue: are you a specialist, or a generalist? Business consultants pitching for work among therapists would suggest that focusing on a specific aspect of mental health is the way to go (Gottlieb, 2012). It may make our hair stand on end, but then it wasn't so long ago that I said I would *never* text a client, or work through the internet. Texting has now become commonplace in society and I will text occasionally, for instance responding to a request for a change of appointment times. I also use the internet and have engaged in regular online sessions with a client living at a distance. I am holding out on 'branding' or employing a consultant, but who knows what I might consider in the future when such an approach has been 'normalised'. Branding may run counter to my belief system as a psychotherapist, but I also recognise the need to attract customers if I want to work. I can only hope that word of mouth, personal integrity and a 'generalised' approach to life's difficulties are what pull me through.

Facing the pressures

Money is a reality: we all need it, and in our society often how good we feel about ourselves is reflected in our ability to make a living. Therapists, I believe, are no exception. In Freud's view, the expense of analysis is 'excessive only in appearance'. He continues:

> Quite apart from the fact that no comparison is possible between restored health and efficiency on the one hand and a moderate financial outlay on the other, when we add up the unceasing costs of nursing-homes and medical treatment and contrast them with the increase of efficiency and earning capacity which results from a successfully completed analysis, we are entitled to say that the patients have made a good bargain. Nothing in life is so expensive as illness – and stupidity.
>
> (Freud, 1995b, p. 371)

Patients *must* pay for their treatment as an act of respect towards the therapist, a measure of the value placed upon what they are receiving.

The one regret most therapists expressed when reflecting back on personal crises, either emotional or physical, they had faced while working was that they had returned to work too soon, most of them for financial reasons. They could not afford to take more time out, particularly those who work almost solely in private practice. As one therapist revealed, all his salary from working within the country's health service went towards paying his mortgage and the regular domestic bills. His private practice, on top of his fulltime job, was what allowed the family to go on holiday, eat dinner out occasionally and pay for the children's few extracurricular activities. As Guy (1987) points out, a therapist's monthly income can fluctuate enormously:

> This is worrisome not only for the therapist, but for the spouse as well. It is very challenging to live within a budget which must constantly adjust for the uncontrollable fluctuations in income ... In the worst of cases, this concern may give rise to not so subtle pressure to earn more money, develop a greater number of referrals, and prolong terminations with dependable clients. The marital tensions and stress which may be caused by this kind of financial insecurity can have a markedly detrimental effect on the marriage. (p. 114)

Ben, a Canadian psychoanalytic therapist, admitted he returned to work too soon due to financial pressures when his partner, also a therapist, suffered a psychotic breakdown. An otherwise very contained man, Ben was evidently struggling with his emotions in the interview, turning his head away and avoiding eye contact with me. He asked himself the question, 'I had to come into work, but ... is there some sign in your work that you're less attentive, you know, when you feel you'd rather be at home?' He went on to ask:

> Do you become alert to difficulties in people of a similar kind? I hope ... but you never know, maybe it's hope more than reality. I hope I've become more sensitive to [the] kind of impact of things on people ... I think that's quite likely. I mean, I hope so and, you think to yourself, well, where there's positive there's [also] negative.

When it all goes wrong

A friend said to me once that he thought money wasn't a problem in a marriage until there was a problem in the marriage. This may be a gross simplification, but the truth is that often money becomes the battleground for other, less well articulated or defined, struggles within the partnership – power dynamics or child care, for instance. In good times, the couple might work well together to sort out and manage these marital strains. However, working as a therapist can lead to formidable unresolved tensions which, in turn, will affect our clinical work. Somehow the expectation within most of us is that, at the very least, we can keep our own house in order and, when we cannot, we wonder how we can possibly serve our clients well. Again, feelings of shame often interfere, afraid that word of our circumstances will spread and we will be found to be human after all, as vulnerable as anyone else to the strains of keeping a marriage together. In his moving account of how divorce from his therapist wife impacted his work with patients, Schlachet (2001) says:

> Never mind the pain of my separation and impending divorce; beyond the misery with my changed circumstances was the nagging feeling that I was perhaps in some way culpable, that these events represented some profound shortcoming of my own which my patients would surely discern, or about which they would at least query me. Not only was the searing shame which such thoughts evoked a source of intense distress, but how could I now help my patients with their relationships when beset by doubts that I could sustain my own? (p. 141)

Divorce is so prevalent in this day and age that, for many people who have not suffered through the process, it may be difficult to understand the deep trauma it can be, regardless of how lonely, violent or strained the marriage was. Rea, a humanistic therapist who finally, and abruptly, ended her marriage of twenty years, made the decision not to see couples during the initial period of her separation and subsequent divorce. 'I knew that I would be likely to encourage them to break up, thereby justifying my own actions,' she said, adding that she had witnessed colleagues who had done just that. 'I didn't want to use clients in that way, so I just stopped taking referrals for couples' work and I didn't take on anyone I knew was dealing with marriage problems as their primary issue. I just couldn't do it, and more than that, I knew I shouldn't do it.'

Rea was perhaps wiser than she knew. Schlachet (2001) describes what it was like for him working while in the midst of his divorce:

> Memories of bitter scenes and confrontations would interpose themselves, especially when patients spoke about related matters. A patient described a fight with her husband: I recalled a particularly bitter one with my wife. Then the immense challenge of seeing the scene through her eyes, of not identifying with the husband, would erupt! It required of me the most resolute concentration, the most intense energy, even a certain amount of affective isolation, in order to continue the work at all in a reasonably balanced manner. (p. 146)

Once again, though, a common experience may also open up the therapist to a deeper empathic connection, according to Gina, a CBT therapist:

> I think you're able to identify with someone. There's almost a part that makes you want to say, well I know exactly what you're going through because I'm going through that at the moment. Of course, I didn't do that, but I think it's probably more about the identifying where that person could be because you're experiencing something similar, whereas maybe someone with a different problem you may not have so much firsthand experience.

Most therapists, however, told me of finding it 'hard to concentrate', or of being only 'half there' while working with patients during their marital break-ups. Rupert, a psychoanalyst, spoke with deep sadness of his experience while working with a particularly damaged patient, 'you really feel in your gut and think my God, I'm coping with this myself, can I work with this guy?'

The stresses of home life are not confined to separation and divorce, of course, and though Johansen (1993) is writing specifically about the trauma of divorce, he perhaps illustrates what any therapist facing difficulties in their personal life might have to contend with while working:

Chronic fatigue, the loss of energy that accompanies prolonged interruption of sleep, and changes in appetite take a toll on the therapist's sense of optimism about the possibility of change. He or she becomes much more vulnerable to the patient's sense of pessimism about the possibility of change and easily identifies with the patient's doubts. The therapist may then be tempted to join the patient's resistance rather than to analyse it. It certainly seems less demanding at moments when little energy is available to the therapist. The cynicism that follows easily undermines the patient's efforts to change. All of this can easily operate at an unconscious level for both patient and therapist.

(Johansen, 1993, p. 95)

Regardless of whether we manage to keep our partnerships intact, personal crisis will inevitably intervene at one time or another. No matter how solid the relationship, no matter how good our kids are or how robust our practice, life cannot possibly be lived without incident or stress. At one time or another we are all struck by the unexpected in life, or even the predictable that we have tried to face off or postpone. We cling to difficult relationships, borrow more on our credit cards and convince ourselves that we can keep going, all with a diminishing sense of confidence that we can manage life at all, let alone well. We are psychotherapists after all, with 'insider knowledge' – how could this possibly be happening to *us?*

But it does, and will continue to do so. Only by admitting, at least to ourselves, that we are human can we begin to acknowledge the impact our psychological state has on our work with clients and patients. Distress at home may open our empathic 'valves' to our clients' states, but it may also close us off when personal anxieties stretch us to extremes. We may cling to our patients for financial security, or seek personal gratification and narcissistic reward in our therapeutic 'successes'. We may avoid what is most painful in our client in order to avoid the pain within ourselves. We may be therapists, but we are also humans. As Beckett say, 'You're on earth. There's no cure for that' (1958, p. 68).

8   The pain of loss

Death in the family

Many years ago, while having coffee with my mother, I asked her if she had been depressed after the death of my sister. 'I wasn't depressed,' she said with a terrible poignancy, 'I was very, very sad.'

In that moment she looked extremely young and suddenly frightened, as if even to speak of my sister's death, now over forty years in the past, was enough to stir in her the terror of unspeakable loss. Her hands shook and she was trying not to cry, excusing herself by naming the early onset of Parkinson's. She was then silent for a few minutes before offering me a small smile, once again covering over this deepest of wounds with her usual social grace. We did not speak of it again.

But I believe my mother articulated something all of us struggle with – the limitations of language – particularly when longing to define the subtleties of experience. In my mother's case, she reserved the word 'depression' to describe a later period of her life, when she was raising five children, two of whom were still in diapers, and we were relatively short of money while my father continued his medical studies.

In previous chapters I have discussed the impact of having children, of facing illness and dealing with depression and/or anxiety. But death, too, comes to us all, and to our partners and children, and we are often deeply affected by the death of friends, people close to us who give us purpose and meaning in our personal lives.

Bearing the unbearable

Several years ago one of my brothers faced the agony of losing his three-year-old son after a sudden illness. In the midst of what appeared to be a bad bout of flu, David had a seizure, fell into a coma from which he did not recover and, a few days later, he died. Having been initially contacted that he was ill, I then received a call to say the hospital ethics committee was meeting to determine whether or not the little boy's life support system should be turned off. He was showing no signs of brain activity. This was not a child I knew well – we are a far-flung family and I don't always see my nieces and nephews as often as I would like – but I know and love my brother and I was devastated at the news.

I immediately booked a flight and telephoned all of my clients to explain that due to an unexpected family crisis I would be away for at least a week. I would ring when I returned to let them know I was back working.

Along with two other siblings I arrived in Canada just a few hours after my nephew's death, to find my brother reeling from the unbelievable events of the past couple of days. Caught in a vortex of confusion, anguish and disbelief, the family moved through the funereal rituals of the following week. It was the middle of a terrible Canadian prairie winter. The earth by the grave was frozen solid, the air so cold we could hardly breathe.

'I always thought if something like this happened to me, I wouldn't survive,' my brother said to me a few days after the funeral, gasping for breath, his whole expression one of deep, unbearable pain, 'But I have done. I'm still alive.'

Emmylou Harris sings, 'and the hardest part is knowing I'll survive', in the painful knowledge that her life will continue despite her grief. No more than that, perhaps, but my brother was 'still alive', carrying the terrible burden of the loss of his precious child. And he had returned to work, not even taking a few more days off following the funeral. How could he possibly spend the time at home, the house empty with his other children at school and his wife managing her grief in her own way too, surrounded by her extended and loving family?

Barbara Chasen (2001), returning to work as a therapist only two weeks after the sudden death of her son, says, 'Freud was right about the nature of productive work: at least for a time that I was in session, I could escape a little from the horror of what my life had become' (p. 7).

Paul, another of my brothers, also wrote (Adams, 2003) of the distress he and his wife suffered during their baby's unexpected illness. He could be speaking for anyone facing the sudden and life-threatening illness of a loved one:

> What is happening to us is as much physical as emotional. Like the turbulence on a plane, when you begin the drop and wonder if there will be an end to it. Except that we are falling not out of the sky but somehow out of ourselves – evacuated, leaving our bodies behind. There is not even the physical presence of our sick child to caress. Our boy is out of sight, out of our control, beyond our understanding. There is nothing we can do to help ourselves, and we are of no help to

him. How could a husband and wife be closer – or more alone? Like physical pain, the distress can be experienced only by a solitary being. Yet it is common pain, or at least parallel, a syncopation of ghastly instants. (2003, pp. 38–39)

These are experiences that in the moment are devoid of reasoning, beyond any possibility of reaching out beyond ourselves. In the death or illness of a child or loved one, we are caught in the incontractable instant of our own terror and grief. We are paralysed.

These are also the crises in life from which we never truly recover, though gradually they become part of the fabric of our day-to-day living, removed from the immediate tragedy and yet ever present; the constant, underground gnawing at the heart that means we are forever different from the person we were before.

As therapists, in the 'moment' of these crises we cannot possibly work. We cannot even 'pretend' to sit in a chair and face another. But, like Chasen, we may soon *need* to work and further, as Gina argues, it is this very texture to our lives which *on reflection* and as we move into another future for ourselves, we can use in our therapeutic relationships. In his sublime treatise on 'loneliness', Moustakas (1961) wrote:

> loneliness is a condition of human life, an experience of being human which enables the individual to sustain, extend, and deepen his humanity. Man is ultimately and forever lonely whether his loneliness is the exquisite pain of the individual living in isolation or illness, the sense of absence caused by a loved one's death, or the piercing joy experienced in triumphant creation. I believe it is necessary for every person to recognize his loneliness, to become intensely aware that, ultimately, in every fibre of his being, man is alone – terribly, utterly alone. (p. xi)

Moustakas, a humanistic clinician and researcher, wrote his book following a personal crisis: he and his wife were forced to decide whether or not to allow a life-threatening operation to go ahead on their daughter. Without it, she would certainly die, but there was also a chance her life would end abruptly on the operating table. His daughter survived, and in the aftermath of such personal distress, he began to explore the loneliness of others. As time passed, he also began to see the acceptance of such personal loneliness as a gift. 'This recognition and meaningful awareness of myself as an utterly lonely person opened the way to deeper human bonds and associations and to a fuller valuing of all aspects of life and nature' (Moustakas, 1961, p. xii).

Illness and death of a partner

Death does not always happen in an instant. There can be many months, years even, while the loved one's health deteriorates. Gerald works as a counsellor within the Canadian school system. He spent a long period of time caring for his partner, in a kind of emotional limbo where returning home at the end of the day was not so much a refuge as a reawakening of dread:

> It's all a blur, but I know that it was sort of like going to work and trying to balance going home and thinking what's it gonna be like when you get home, what's happened, you know, that ... you're completely stressed out, and I suppose, like you mentioned before, going to work sometimes was a relief, just to get away from that, but then when you're counselling, and you're dealing with other people's pain, it's sort of don't always ... it sort of then reminds you of what you're going through, though sometimes it was good because it made me realise that I wasn't the only one going through something, you know, there's a lot of young kids who are dealing with some really horrendous stuff too, so I think, you know, I got strength out of the counselling too.

This common impulse to escape into work may impose a demand on our clients and patients to 'benefit' from our work with them. Why would we want to 'escape' into work if there was no satisfaction to be gained there? Sandy, a therapist who acknowledged a lengthy and ongoing battle with alcohol, illustrates how this may sometimes play out:

> Often times when I'm working, I'm in a completely different space. I'm not in my life. I'm in somebody else's life and so I find that the hour sort of flies by and hopefully, most of the time, I feel like I've done something and actually both of us, I hope, leave the session feeling more energised and soul lifted.

If we are clinging to our work in order to soothe ourselves, is this a positive, or a negative? When does this help our clients, as therapists often claim, through our increased capacity to understand or empathise, and when does it inhibit our work, unconsciously shifting the focus from them onto ourselves in an attempt to find relief from our personal traumas?

In my view, everyone needs to be needed and working as psychotherapists may, for some of us, be particularly satisfying on this front. Siobhan, a psychoanalytic therapist, lost her husband several years ago. 'I've often felt I'm in a rather worse state than people in front of me at times, and it's very interesting about how you use that, or how you find yourself being used through it, using it yourself.' Siobhan went on to say that at times, before her bereavement, she had sometimes felt she lived in a 'different world' than her patients but, when her husband died, 'I certainly didn't … we were in pain together'. She believes she could then sit with a 'lot more pain as opposed to anxiety'. She is convinced that the experience, as painful and terrible as becoming a widow was, has made her a 'better therapist'. She went on to say, 'Had my husband lived for the next 10 years, I don't think I'd be the same therapist.'

How is it that a therapist can be in so much personal pain, and yet so open to the suffering of others? Siobhan's conviction rests in the belief that her own sorrow provided her with a greater capacity for containing their pain. Is it, perhaps, that in the midst of such personal loss, as in Chasen's (2001) case, or in Siobhan's, we cannot close ourselves up in a defence against pain. We embody it, we are nothing but the pain, and in those moments we can be used by our patients to make sense of themselves, to provide something of a mirror of how such trauma and loss can actually be survived. Like Moustakas (1961) and his recognition that his profound loneliness had value, perhaps our clients sometimes need to recognise this in us too.

Wynona is an experienced therapist who divides her working week between a public mental health service in the centre of Calgary and a small private practice at her home in the suburbs. Her relationship with her father was often difficult. However, when he died she experienced a deep grief and sadness, a more straightforward response than usual where her father was concerned.

> I'd always experienced sadness that was complicated by anger or anxiety or attachment or something else, and it was … I just … when I experienced it, I thought this is something new for me to learn and then I can take that into my work! That was my positive spin on the situation. I said, God I really know what this feels like now, this feels really different to anything else I've ever experienced. It's more painful, very painful, but it isn't complicated … well I had a less complicated grief. I know other people have very complicated grief reactions, but I was … you know, I guess that's what I mean when I say [I am] a work in progress. I imagine that other experiences might have those sorts of effects, and I feel you just kind of get an extra layer, as you get older, you just layer on insight as you get older, at least that's my view.

Wynona illustrates that our knowledge builds over time, layer upon layer, not just through training, or as a result of our histories, but current events give our lives texture and additional understanding into the experience of others.

Overwhelming tide of events

Pauline is an integrative psychotherapist working in the north of England. Over a period of five years she was faced with the death of her closest friend, her partner's life-threatening illness and her mother's descent into Alzheimer's, where the parent she once knew was no longer visible behind the unpredictability of her disease. In Pauline's case she took a leave of absence, without pay, in order to deal with and process her difficult experience. Although this option may not be open to everyone, she believes this is what saved her:

> The hardest thing for me during that time was coping with the terror because I did feel as if, in terms of my personal constellation of people that mattered, all the most significant ... figures in my life were going, or were threatened – my best friend, my partner, my mother, and I literally felt – really literally – as if the ground was dissolving. You know there were times when I would get this mental image of life sort of draining through a dark hole, literally sort of dissolving down a dark hole, and there were certain key moments such as when [my partner] became ill again, the ground seemed to dissolve ... and I could remember just that feeling of everything disappearing and so I think my preoccupation during that time was how do I deal with this terror, how do I either stop myself going back into the past or projecting into the future, and it literally was a day by day, really inch by inch, learning in how to stay in the present, and how to access support, largely support at a spiritual level, largely really focusing on what I experienced as help. I'm not religious but I do have a very sort of strong, very strong sort of spiritual infrastructure and it was time I started to look at it, and it was time I started to really integrate it into my life and I needed to do it fast and I did, I did do it.

Returning to work she felt better fortified to manage her feelings within the therapy room, to engage in other people's pain and manage some of the difficult transferential elements that arise within the therapeutic encounter. We need, in order to manage the complex requirements of engaging in psychotherapy, to be robust, open to the vicissitudes of our patients and both their conscious and unconscious attacks. We need to be strong enough, in a Winnicottian sense, to be able to bear both our own and our patients' hatred (Winnicott, 1947).

As Pauline illustrated, it isn't just the illness and death of direct family members that may cause us grief, but friends too. Bernadette suffered a series of three deaths in a single month, all of them close friends. She said,

And I kind of was in work, but I wasn't really ... I was kind of ... I was there ... I was a body. I wasn't really doing much more than being a body in front of the client for probably two weeks I'd say ... because my mind wasn't there. I couldn't think, so I couldn't think clearly, especially when one client brought up her fear of her parents dying, and although my deaths weren't parental – I was lucky – but they were very close friends and so I really I couldn't go there.

Bernadette went on to say that she did not believe her clients were aware of her personal struggle, but the director of the clinic certainly was: 'He sent me home one day, but that was after I saw the client. I went home. The rest of the day was clear so I went home after I'd seen the client, and I had time off to go the funerals.'

The opportunity to grieve is an important issue here. Attending funerals, and a period of time to recover and process the grief is essential, a difficult thing when working within a medical setting where time off for grieving is usually limited, in some cases restricted to just two weeks, and usually only in connection with a close relative. The death of friends is not usually taken into account as having such personal significance. Bernadette added, 'They don't allow you to have time off unless it's a close relative, so would I have managed it differently? I think in an ideal world I would have done. I would have had time out for about a week or two weeks.'

Reflection

Is a therapist's personal suffering like a muscle, then, that once stretched and, after some discomfort, may provide us with more flexibility, or an increase in stamina? This awakens questions of the 'wounded healer', and whether or not therapists need to know suffering in the course of their working lives. It is not the absence of life's traumas that may provide for therapists' ability to connect with their patients, but rather the opposite.

Bereavement sits at the core of so many therapists' lives, the loss of children, partners and parents, and of friends too, perhaps sometimes not recognised generally as a deep trauma from which someone might need time to recover. Ultimately, these experiences may mean a therapist avoids that which might be personally painful, but it may also provide the therapist with a more profound understanding of the immediacy of pain surrounding terror and loss, particularly in the case of trauma where the pain may be as acute today as it was at the time of the event, in the words of Faulkner, 'The past is never dead. It's not even past' (1951, act 1, sc. 3).

9 A problem shared...

Psychotherapy these days may often be predicated on science and research, but I believe at its heart it is truly an 'art'. Like Edvard Munch, I believe that it is born out of both 'joy and sorrow, but mostly sorrow'. No matter what defensive measures we take, no matter how hard we work to avoid pain, life will invariably develop texture. Even in the womb we are exposed to parental behaviour and tensions. After birth we thrive, or not, according to our mother's capacity to attend and attune to us. Life goes on, every moment along the way adding new pieces to the puzzle of our lives which either reinforce or shift our view of the world.

This book explores the impact of our personal lives on our work with clients and patients. In this chapter I focus on some of the points touched upon in previous chapters: the importance of supervision in maintaining 'good health' within our therapeutic relationships and the fundamental requirement that we have a productive life outside the office too. What are a few of the warning signs when the balance is tipped and we might find ourselves on the wrong side of good practice? When do we rationalise what we cannot justify in order to give in to unhealthy impulses? Is there any way to overcome, or override, shame? Like any artist, it takes courage to speak with your own voice, to create something that is not simply a pastiche of what has come before you. Not everyone is an innovator, of course, but through personal bravery, creativity and authentic expression, we can all develop as therapeutic 'artists' in our own right. Without heart, creative discipline and the exercising of good practice, all the theory in the world is rendered meaningless.

Supervision

Creativity cannot happen in isolation. A painter needs a subject and, if the work is to have a life beyond the studio, gallery owners and patrons must be involved. Even Van Gogh had his brother. Musicians need other musicians and writers need a life and relationships from which they can extract detail and emotional resonance. Actors need a director, and a director needs a play. Transformation of the mundane into the sublime is often a collective exercise, an exchange of ideas, reciprocity with others out of which something beautiful and meaningful may emerge. Even hermits have gods, or their surroundings, about which they contemplate. Beauty is the product of eyes upon another, a person or an object, a view of a small piece of the world. I look from my window and I see the sea, 'the lonely sea and the sky'.[1]

For psychotherapists to work we need clients and patients, and we need supervisors to ensure that in the complexity of the dynamic we are not losing sight of either ourselves or our clients. Perhaps I should say we need supervisors to ensure that we do not lose sight of ourselves and therefore lose sight of our patients. The therapist with a history of rescuing others will likely wish to rescue her client, and one with issues of powerlessness may well struggle with a client's sense of autonomy. Those with a tendency towards external, narcissistic gratification will seek it in their patients. This is regardless of experience. In times of stress we fall back into familiar patterns. Within a good supervisory relationship these 'default' positions may be noted and checked, explored and reckoned with.

Therapists in my study cited supervision as the most important aspect of their professional support, and for many it was a long-standing relationship of many years. For other therapists peer supervision was their solid base, meeting regularly and for some mixing a set time of formal contact followed by social engagement, such as dinner together or a visit to the pub.

Both supportive and stretching, supervision is an opportunity to work creatively in exploring the therapist's own process in relation to their clinical work. The supervisory relationship is fundamental to good practice and in most places it is also an ethical requirement, whether it is provided by a supervisor with whom the therapist has no other contact, group supervision or regular meetings with a peer, an arrangement formalised between colleagues to meet and discuss clinical work. What matters is that it is robust and challenging, non-blaming and exploratory, containing and unambiguous.

Looking for the 'right' supervisor

What do you look for in a supervisor?

Early in my counselling training (person-centred) I needed a supervisor who could also 'teach' me, reassure me that I was 'getting it right' and, when I was not, soothe and encourage me to learn from my mistakes. I was lucky. My supervisor had a sense of humour and, considering my theoretical shortfall, she valued my personal qualities. As Carroll argues, during this early stage of a therapist's development 'education is more at the heart of supervision than is counselling' (1996, p. 27).

On reflection, this supervisor managed the erratic nature of my development with great skill. On any given day I could be high as a kite with confidence, a miracle worker – after only a few sessions a client had often 'really shifted' – or I was plunged into gloom at the impossibility of it all, my client was 'stuck' and there was nothing I could 'do'. This supervisor suggested reading, invited me to look at my clients in context and to some degree explored a few of my personal issues in relation to them. She encouraged me to use my personal therapy to look even more deeply into what my clients might be evoking in me.

My training moved on into integrative psychotherapy and I found a new supervisor. Formidable and challenging, the 'educating' continued and the inquiry into my own process deepened. Supervision here was rarely comfortable, but it was always educational. By now I had a little more theory under my belt and so the complexities of the therapeutic relationship were explored more extensively. I no longer believed in the miracle of instant 'shifts' and I began to appreciate the power of transference and counter-transference, my own contribution to eruptions in the work. While I worked individually with this supervisor, I also attended a day-long 'group' supervision session with her once a month. To say that this group process was stimulating, challenging and informative is a great understatement. Sometimes one or another member left and a new one arrived, but a hard core of us continued even after qualifying. I would be hard put now to say which was more valuable to my development as a therapist: my formal training, or the group and individual supervision. They were at least equal.

Eventually, I moved off to undertake postgraduate psychoanalytic training, necessitating a new supervisor – the person with whom I still work. In this relationship the 'educational' element is conducted more in the form of mutual discussion and exploration. Perhaps I have grown up as a therapist, or maybe his approach is simply different. Regardless, without this regular support I know my clients would suffer. Another pair of ears and eyes, a difference of perspective and exploration of the transference and counter-transferential elements are a constant source of inspiration and insight. As Mollon points out: 'One function of supervision of psychotherapy is the creation of a space for thinking. The thinking is not linear, logical "left-brain" cognition, but a kind of free-associative mulling over' (1997, p. 33). And it is within this space that creativity can develop. Ideas are explored, my mind wanders into previously closed-off internal spaces and I see my patient anew, within the context of their history perhaps, but importantly within the context of my own and a view to what we have created together.

Therapists are human too!

I was lucky; I trawled around just enough to find the right supervisor, one who was a good fit for me. In each case I followed a trail. My first supervisor lived close by, was on the list of named supervisors for my training course and she had space at a time that suited me. The second supervisor I had seen in action within the Institute in which I was training and where she had previously been on staff. I liked what I saw – she was a little scary but warm enough that I knew I could work with her, and so I made contact. She was also a North American living in London, which on reflection may have been important. I am an immigrant, with particular sensibilities and attitudes developed in the cradle. Unconsciously I may have believed that on some basic level I would be understood without always having to explain myself, like a child's need for intuitive understanding.

I had early contact with the third supervisor when arranging for him to give a seminar. I found him knowledgeable and approachable and as a result contacted him later to ask if he had spaces for one more supervisee.

This sounds simple but, like the relationship between therapist and client, a good fit is important and not just anyone will do. We may need different supervisors at different stages of our development as psychotherapists. This is not to negate what has come before, but to move forward and explore new aspects of ourselves and gain different perspectives. Every supervisor will have a different way of viewing client presentation and 'pathology', even within the same approach.

Shame: an inhibitor to good practice

Ronnestad and Orlinsky, considering both the negative and positive aspects of supervision, show that 'practitioners at all experience levels, theoretical orientations, professions, and nationalities report that supervised client experience is highly important for their current and career development' (2009, p. 188). However, as they also point out, a 'negative' supervisory experience can undermine a therapist's confidence, particularly in the early stages of their professional development. Allowances for fundamental mistakes (running over time, tendencies to over self-disclose or defensively withdraw) all need to be understood within the context of the therapist's development and stage of training. It is their integrity that is important and their fundamental understanding and acceptance of ethical practice. Theoretical knowledge is built upon, layer by layer, as is professional confidence and the awareness that mistakes and confusion are all part of what goes into creating the working alliance.

Shame is always in the mix, though admittedly I may be speaking from my own perspective. However, everyone suffers elements of shame somewhere within themselves and as Nathanson points out:

Often what we encounter is shame affect experienced not even as anything we might call shame but as a reaction pattern determined by the point on the compass of shame made natural by the way each of us has travelled through time to develop our attitude toward shame affect. (1987, p. 459)

The supervisory relationship is like a Petri dish, toxic cultures of shame and vulnerability often fusing into defensive mulch. Trainee psychotherapists imagine that experienced therapists always get it right and experienced therapists think they should get it right. How often have I heard clients training as therapists express the fear that I will break confidentiality and report them to their training institutes as unfit to practice? This must also be true with those who come to me for supervision, though interestingly that anxiety has never been articulated. I can't believe that they all feel so secure with me that old terrors don't surface at least occasionally, particularly when I am poking and prodding them about the personal and uncomfortable aspects of their work.

Shame and defensiveness are also symptoms, warning signs that something needs to be considered, even while there is a powerful drive to keep it to ourselves. Shame stands in the way of creativity; it inhibits and drives the best part of us underground. Through the insidious nature of shame the potential for good erupts in a corruption of the therapeutic relationship, through crossing ethical boundaries and giving in to impulse, using the work as an arena to exert power rather than to encourage liberation and autonomy. In these cases we use our personal difficulties to discharge anxiety and gain short-term relief, all at the expense of our vulnerable patients.

If it is incumbent on the supervisor to hold to the boundaries by example, so is it a responsibility on the part of the supervisee to allow themselves to be questioned, challenged and prompted to reflect, most importantly in those hidden corners of ourselves we would prefer not see. Defensiveness, on the part of either the supervisee or the supervisor, is a signal that something has been touched upon that is worth looking at.

Supervision as 'relationship'

With my second supervisor, we had to juggle a bit, getting to know one another because, although we had had previous contact, she pointed out during our initial assessment session that she didn't really 'know' me. Our relationship had to develop before I could settle into trust and safety, bring those elements of 'failure' and vulnerability in my work that might cause me shame. I admired her enormously, as a clinician and as a teacher and this inhibited me at the beginning. If she was so good, did this mean I was not so good? Could I ever be as effective, as knowledgeable, or as confident as she was? I suspect now that she was not nearly as confident as I imagined her to be, but she *was* knowledgeable and I have no doubt at all that she was an effective clinician. The proof was in her ability to form positive and challenging supervisory relationships, in her faith in each member of the group and her dedication in encouraging us to reflect on our own process in relation to *every* client, not just those who stimulated uncomfortable feelings, but those who also evoked in us pleasurable sensations of 'achievement'. I blush to think of the number of times I presented clinical work hoping for once to be able to focus on my 'success', only for her to query that very complacency, forcing me to look more deeply into my own need to have my client become 'well' or 'improve'. It is from her that I finally learned that one day I might be a psychotherapist, but I was never going to be a miracle worker. And no matter how much theory I had under my belt, if I wasn't prepared to look within, I was never going to help anyone else understand or manage their internal world either. If I wasn't prepared to think creatively about my clients and about myself in relation to them ... well, I wasn't prepared to follow that train of thought. There was nothing for it but to take constant measure.

The obvious value of group supervision is the contribution of others, particularly within an 'integrative' frame where each member practices from a different therapeutic tradition, or a synthesis of models. But even within a singular approach, every participant will consider clinical work from their own idiosyncratic position. And, as within a healthy therapy group, the group dynamic is exactly what helps to bring about a change of perspective, thereby promoting healthier relationships with others. In my view, there is little difference within a supervision group. As Yalom points out, personal pathology will always play out (1995, p. 28). It needn't be stated, it will be enacted. The group format allows the 'rescuer' to show himself, along with the 'pragmatist' and the 'controller'. 'Victims' don't escape, nor do elements of grandiosity, in my experience inherent to some degree in *every* therapist – why ever else would you believe you can do this job?

For me the most meaningful aspect of the group supervision process was containment of my shame, which surfaced all too often in relation to my work when it was not going 'well'. This played out over and over again with the client who eventually took out the complaint – my supervisor saw it coming from a long way off. Caught between a rock and a hard place, I did not know how to withdraw from the work, nor how to 'progress', which was impossible. It was from this group that I received such support, even after we had disbanded and we met individually rather than collectively. They knew me and they knew my work, my strengths and my weaknesses. In front of them at least, I could express the depth of my fear and shame. By this time the meetings might be considered 'peer' supervision. Gilbert and Evans (2000) stress the importance of peer contact:

> After qualification, peer group supervision may also form an important part in a psychotherapist's support system. We have found that once people no longer have the support of an ongoing training group, gaining sufficient professional support becomes a challenge and a necessity. Peer supervision can provide some of this support, since a peer will be experiencing many similar stresses, joys and challenges. We have come to regard regular contact of this kind as essential to the well-being of a psychotherapist in the demanding professional climate in which we operate. (p. 81)

I have pictures of our supervision group: our graduation and, a few years later, a dinner to celebrate the end of our work together. In both pictures we are all smiling, huddled together as if for warmth, arms draped over one another like a high school photo. Knowing one another so well, these friendships will never die, we seem to be saying. Like war buddies we exude a louche confidence. Within a few years, I had survived the professional complaint, one had moved abroad and since then so has another. One of us has given up working and someone else has experienced a series of very painful bereavements. Several have faced bouts of ill health, forcing them to take time out. In one way or another since those few lovely, and glorious, moments of confidence on both occasions, we have all been proven human. Again.

Supervision as collusion

No matter how potentially good the supervisor is, they will only be as good as we allow them to be.

A colleague recently bemoaned the fact that she could not find a supervisor, nor could she settle into a peer group or peer arrangement. 'I'm just not finding the right person,' she huffed. The conversation moved on and a few minutes later she admitted she had not been in supervision for nearly two years.

This was a therapist who, even before we had graduated, had developed a very busy private practice, advertising herself as a specialist in just about everything – an A to Z therapist who stretched through the alphabet on her website offering bereavement counselling, coaching, organisational consultancy and working with eating and personality disorders, to name just a few. There wasn't an aspect of life she didn't cover, or at least not one I could think of. This meant, of course, that her clients ranged from the 'healthy unwell' to the 'deeply disturbed' and she admitted when we spoke that she was seeing a number of complex patients about whom she had not yet consulted with anyone – including, in at least one case, the psychiatric team who were still monitoring her client's condition.

She must have noticed my expression. 'Look, I'm okay. I'm experienced, and I've had loads of therapy over the years.' She waved a hand in the air and sounded positively breezy, crossing her legs and sipping her decaff latte. 'I just can't find a supervisor who's as experienced as me, or knows as much as I do. And they never seem to understand my approach, my particular way of working.'

I was virtually speechless, not quite sure how to penetrate such a solid shield of over-confidence. I noticed she didn't suggest a round of peer supervision with me, to carry her through until she did find a supervisor who suited her. Clearly, I wasn't her professional equal either. Instead of challenging her I muttered something like, 'that must be difficult'. She looked victorious. I slunk away feeling both superior (I use supervision!), but envious too (I wish I had that kind of confidence!). But more than anything I understood that this was a colleague to whom I would never refer anyone and, as soon as I found my voice again, I would need to find the courage to challenge her regarding the ethical requirements of good practice. I also felt an enormous sadness that the profession itself was being degraded through her failure to adhere to one of the basic requirements. Who was there to monitor her impulses, challenge her rationalisations or make sense of her counter-transference? These are difficult enough to deal with in discussion with a colleague or supervisor, let alone on our own.

Not finding the 'right' supervisor after trying out a few may mean that we are looking for collusion rather than challenge, soothing rather than exploration and complacency rather than insight. And there will be supervisors who find it easier to allow grandiosity to thrive rather than delve into the untidy corners where the underlying truth of our vulnerability and humanity might reside. They will be supervisors with an investment in maintaining their own grandiose position. There is nothing like shining one another's mirror to keep the illusion intact.

Supervision is only as good as we allow it to be. And there may be only one basic rule: if you don't want to bring it to supervision, you probably should. This could invite feelings of shame, exposing ourselves to difficult counter-transference issues: erotic attraction and sexual fantasies, anger, dislike, visceral hatred, boredom, 'forgetting' the client, missed appointments, over self-disclosure, wanting to be liked, rescuing ... the list is endless. The supervisor's role is to help us explore these responses, to delve into their meaning and find a way to understand, rather than to act upon them. What we feel in response to a client is never wrong, but how we *act* as a result can be. Supervision is containment: we contain the patient, but the supervisor acts as a container to the therapist. The supervisor in turn has their supervision, and it continues before rounding back again, a virtuous circle.

Note

1   Masefield, J. (1902), 'Sea Fever', *Salt-water Poems and Ballads*. New York: Macmillan.

10 Finally

Letting go of the myth

In the heart of a story, the truth resides. As a journalist I was always more interested in the stories than the 'facts'. During the miners' strike in Britain during the early 1980s, I was far more absorbed by how the families were faring than I was in how much money the mining companies were losing, or the divisive machinations of the political parties of the time. How did these strikers keep going without money or, paradoxically, the coal to fuel their fires during the winter? Did neighbour agree with neighbour about 'sticking it out', or did some want to cross the picket line and return to work simply so they could feed their families? Visiting their houses in those north-eastern coal mining towns, the women all had knitting machines, turning out sweaters that nobody could afford to buy, for most of them an exercise in futility, but at least it was some sort of action, rendering them a little less powerless. Through the possibility of making something to sell, they were keeping hope alive, or at least despair at bay. I have never forgotten those women, their pain and their courage.

Through researching the personal lives of therapists, and the impact on their professional practice, I have been given privileged access into their stories of bravery, stamina, despair and hope. Despite the divisions, real or imagined, between the various traditions and models in which we train, the common denominator is our humanity.

Stemming from my own confusion and pain at various times during my working life, I wanted to find out from colleagues what stresses they had faced and how they had dealt with them. Quite simply, I wanted to learn from them. In the course of speaking to forty therapists, I have discovered many more similarities than differences; the extent of pain within therapists' personal histories and the lengths to which so many have gone to make some meaning out of the early tragedies and traumas of their lives. These psychotherapists are not the exception; I am convinced they are the rule, speaking for a global community of practitioners.

In this chapter I reflect on the process and findings in my study. The purpose of the inquiry was to determine if, and how, therapists believe their experience outside the therapy room affects their work with clients and patients. I explore some of the key points in previous chapters and highlight areas for discussion, not to prove a point, but to stimulate debate which may lead to some understanding (Coles, 1989; Eysenck, 1976; Moustakas, 1990). I reflect on the need for therapists to consider the impact of their personal lives and, in particular, their histories in relation to their clinical work and the need for therapists to support one another, to accept and consider that colleagues may be suffering depression. In a field which purports to work towards the psychological health of others, it is essential that we also promote the good health of our own community. In the end, we are all 'wounded healers' (Sedgwick, 1994).

I also revisit the idea that depression may help us to empathise more deeply in the room with our clients and patients, but anxiety may interfere with that contact. As Norcross and Guy point out, 'The most common precipitating events of distressed psychotherapists are disruptions in their own lives – dysfunctional marriages, serious illnesses, and other interpersonal losses – as opposed to client problems' (2007, p. 53). We are vulnerable on several fronts; it is not just our histories which may intrude on our clinical work, but our current, day-to-day lives too with their endless array of possible difficulties and stresses.

How do we make ourselves more aware of our unconscious processes at work, aspects of ourselves which, by their very nature, may be immediately inaccessible to us, with clarity only possible in hindsight? How does 'pain', both physical and psychological, impact our work, and what challenges are imposed on us as therapists as a result of our histories? That which makes us an effective therapist may also hinder our work under different circumstances and with particular clients. What might it mean to our clients and patients if we are using our work as psychotherapists to replicate or 'fix' what we could not manage as children? When does job satisfaction mean avoidance of particular issues and a gravitation towards others, areas meaningful to ourselves perhaps, but not so crucial to those we work with?

A short summing up

Virtually all the therapists in this study agreed that their personal lives impacted their work with clients and patients. However, one therapist could not identify where that impact might be in his own practice, and another believed it would have an impact only if he disclosed to his client.

Humanistic therapists and those integrative therapists who work mainly within the humanistic tradition also work primarily in the 'here and now'.

Their focus is on the current relationship between therapist and client. However, in this study they were also aware that personal stresses could impact their work and did not deny that historical elements in their history were also likely to have an impact, particularly if denied to their 'awareness'.

Psychoanalytic therapists and those integrative therapists working from this perspective were the most likely to admit to the possibility of unconscious elements in their history and their current lives playing out in the therapy room. Transference and counter-transference are at the crux of their work and the 'working' through of these is considered essential to developing insight and bringing about change in a client's personal relationships.

CBT therapists were more likely to consider current events affecting their work, admitting they found it difficult to work if they were tired or distracted by anxiety. Working within a 'cognitive' frame they were less concerned with unconscious processes and the possibility of historical 'enactments' within the therapy room.

The difference of perspective among therapists rests primarily in their clinical understanding, from the CBT therapist who is concerned with his *current* state of psychological health, to the psychoanalytic therapist who has a deep theoretical investment in the unconscious motivations of both parties in the therapy room.

But what is most striking are the similarities between the various traditions, rather than their few marked differences in theoretical perspective. Every psychotherapist suffers at times, and each one works hard to find a way through. They all, for the most part, hold the good of their patients at heart. They strive to do a good job and they are all vulnerable, particularly those who do not seem able to hold a narrative of their own lives, or suffer shame at the possible exposure of their personal vulnerability. Therapists who unexpectedly experience psychological ill-health within their immediate family appear particularly vulnerable to shame, unable as they are to prevent suffering even in their own home. On the other hand, those therapists who experienced deep psychological disturbance within their families in childhood are often more accepting of their own vulnerability, more likely, though by no means certainly, to seek out therapy for themselves because they know they need it. For these therapists, the need for external support at times is simply an accepted part of their lives.

Bias and considerations

In any research process focusing on narrative rather than 'facts', there will be bias. I began this process with the conviction that the therapist's personal life does affect their work. I am concluding with that belief still intact, if not even more entrenched as a result of the stories I have heard from so many psychotherapists over the past few years. I am also an integrative psychotherapist who works very much from a psychoanalytical perspective. This means that, while I have some theoretical knowledge of other disciplines, my understanding of events and processes is primarily from this perspective. While I have worked hard to hold the 'phenomenological' frame for each therapist I know that, in the end, my conclusions and perspectives on their histories and practices may not always be theirs, but simply a product of my particular interpretation of events.

In the beginning, after an interview in which a therapist found it difficult to reflect on his or her inner process and the impact this might have on their clinical work, or when they spoke of denial, I believed it was a 'bad' interview, much as I would were I reporter working on a specific story. In the event of a news 'piece', I would simply arrange an interview with someone else to compensate for the earlier person's inability to meet the challenge. I am grateful that others wiser than I were able to point out that in research there is no such thing as a 'bad interview' and that all interviews are information. This may seem obvious, but if the question concerns the 'challenges' presented by therapists' personal lives, and the interviewee agrees in principle but shows little aptitude for reflecting how this might be true in their case, it would be so easy to dismiss them rather than take into account what they have to say. In this case, those therapists became the 'one in ten' who found it difficult to reflect on their personal process in relation to their work, a professional shortcoming that I believe should be taken seriously.

Although in most areas there did not appear to be a difference in perspectives or experience amongst the therapeutic traditions, the apparent distinctions between how therapists of different traditions 'cope' with life was particularly meaningful in my view, with CBT practitioners 'managing' their struggles, while at the other end of the spectrum psychoanalytic therapists needing to 'understand' in order to survive. In between lay varying degrees of either approach, or in the case of some humanistic therapists, to express and manage their distress through external or physical means, including body therapy.

Fundamentally, experiences of distress were remarkably similar – including, for example, parenthood and pain, as was the impact these had on their work as practitioners. Depression may have been viewed differently, though this is an educated guess on my part as I did not investigate each therapist's definition of depression. However, psychoanalytic therapists in this study appear to have the lowest rate of depression, and integrative therapists the highest. What accounts for this, other than perhaps each tradition's view of what constitutes depression? Certainly I could hear personal struggle in the stories of psychoanalytic therapists, and sometimes in much the same detail as those of humanistic or integrative therapists who spoke of their distress in terms of 'depression'.

Personal investment

My research interest stemmed from my personal experience with intense anxiety when facing a professional complaint and during which time I continued working. I believed that I had 'bracketed' my distress, keeping it out of the room during my work with clients. In fact, I experienced my hours working as sweet relief from the stress and worry and the persistent (and irrational) fantasy that I would by stripped of my professional credentials and no longer be able to work.

Throughout this period I was also in therapy, a support for which I was, and still am, deeply grateful. I also had the support of colleagues, who rallied round and expressed their confidence in me by continuing to work with me in supervision groups, inviting me to social events and not hesitating to send me a stream of referrals.

Only after the complaint had been dropped did several of my supervisees, who up until then had not known of the complaint, say, 'I knew something was wrong, I just wasn't sure what.' I had not been so successful at bracketing my internal distress as I had believed. There was certainly leakage, but how on earth would I have occupied my time and diverted myself from my anxiety if I had not worked? What would I have needed to put in place?

I wonder how spontaneous I was within the therapy room during those months? Was my thinking light enough to spark connections and stay tuned to what my clients were saying beneath the surface of their words? Outside of the room I was heavy with worry and grief for what I imagined might happen and my loss of self-confidence. As someone generally considered witty, I did not make a quip for months, noticing that laughter had gone only once it returned. What subjects and themes did I gravitate towards because they might lead to an easier process for my client and therefore be more obviously gratifying for me as a result? When did I avoid the difficult, unconscious, beneath-the-surface work that comprises a more complex internal compound and often demands an intense effort in the therapy room, but which may, in the end, make a more pronounced difference in the life of my patient?

Following on from this experience I worked hard to understand some of the unconscious motivations that had led me to continue in this disastrous therapeutic relationship which, in hindsight, was obviously headed towards a professional complaint; this client had a history of litigation both in the workplace and in her personal relationships, often suing her former partners, or neighbours when she felt let down or betrayed (Adams, 2008; Bernier and Kearns, 2007).

> Eileen presented with issues of low self-esteem ('I hate myself') and a comment that her partner of six years thought she was 'crazy'. This, she explained, was because she could not help herself when she was angry. 'I just lose it completely,' she told me in a remarkably cheerful tone of voice. While I did pick up on the unconscious warning that she was likely to 'lose it completely' with me at some stage, I was not attuned to my own unconscious response – in the face of painful attack I historically respond by either withdrawing in shame or by working hard to win the protagonist over. In the first moments of this particular enactment, I made an effort to express warmth and acceptance, two qualities I understood to be fundamental to the therapeutic relationship (Rogers, 1957) but in this instance might also be seen as an attempt to ensure my own safety. I don't believe that it was in the offering of these two 'core conditions' that the enactment resided, but in the paradoxically conscious effort I had to make to provide them. They did not come entirely easily.
>
> (Adams, 2008, p. 49)

Like the therapists I interviewed (working within institutions aside, virtually all of them said they derived enjoyment from their work), I also gain enormous satisfaction from my work as a psychotherapist. However, when is that satisfaction at the expense of my clients, and when is it in the service of my clients? When do I labour to enliven my client in order not to feel the 'death' of my sister through my mother's grief at the death of her child (Green, 1983), and when do I use that primitive and primary experience to empathise and make sense of my client's experience? If, as Frankl (1959) says, suffering is a necessary and unavoidable part of the human experience, how do I make meaning of this in a positive way, rather than in my very human potential for repetition, sublimation and destruction (Freud, 1915)?

Impact on work: the initial question

There were only two therapists in my research who found it difficult to identify where their personal lives might be affecting their work, even though they agreed that it could. While these are extreme cases, perhaps they highlight the tendency in all of us to see what we want to see and perhaps hide what is uncomfortable from ourselves (and others!). Donald, a humanistic therapist, pointed out that we might be more inclined to consider the impact of our personal lives if the outcome is good, than if the effect is negative.

Within the interviews, therapists struggled at times to acknowledge how their distress had entered into the clinical setting. One psychotherapist said, 'I'm not sure that it affected necessarily … I'd like to think it didn't. I know it does a bit … ' and another said point blank, 'I'm great at denial,' when considering her own depression and the impact this might have on her work. She wakes in the morning sometimes praying that 'nobody is too depressed'.

We may be shocked at this direct statement, finding in our judgement a kind of solace that we do not behave in the same way. However, what therapist can deny that there are days when, feeling burdened ourselves, we wished that life as a therapist was easier, that in the therapy room we did not have to tangle with too many demons, and that every client left feeling better so we might feel better ourselves? There are days, perhaps, when we unconsciously avoid digging too deeply for the painful insight that will enrage or leave our client feeling despair rather than comfort, or when we dread our patient playing out, yet again, the corruptions of an abusive childhood?

There is a danger, perhaps, that in our judgement of others we can hide our own vulnerabilities, we can hunker down and convince ourselves that we do not behave in the same way, that we would not let our personal lives *interfere* with our work, using it only for the good of our clients and patients. There is a convenient 'blindness', like blinkers on a horse, that allows us to continue even when we, and our clients, might be better served from taking time out, returning to therapy or taking help in forms that would mean an admission of our struggle: acknowledging that our marriage is in trouble for instance, or accepting a substance abuse problem. As Geller, Norcross and Orlinsky (2005) point out, therapists often struggle to express their vulnerability within their own therapy. And if they are not expressing it in therapy, how much are they admitting to themselves? We know from experience that within the therapy room our clients find relief and clarity through the symbolisation of words, through the very voicing of their distress and finding a narrative, a story to wrap around their experience to give it meaning. Therapists are no different.

If, as Geller, Norcross and Orlinsky (ibid.) claim in their study on therapists' struggle in personal therapy, we are 'threatened by the dilemma of "needing help"'(p. 6), we place ourselves above our clients, a narcissistic position that splices us from the common humanity of those we seek to treat.

Therapists are created, not born, and it is through our histories that we find ourselves unconsciously gravitating, by whatever route, towards the profession. Many of us are 'copers' as Winifred, a humanistic therapist, pointed out, but the 'coper' in us may mean that we are less inclined to ask for help than is healthy, and when we do ask for help from our colleagues, what is the response?

One therapist in this study was so dismayed at her colleague's response to her plea for support that she felt as if she had been slapped. Another therapist, a humanistic practitioner, struggled to find a therapist to support him after a life-threatening accident. He was too well-known within the therapeutic community and no one was inclined to take him on. This was a dilemma expressed by just under a quarter of the therapists in this study, one of them resorting to therapy via Skype in order to preserve confidentiality and distance from the community in which he works.

Wounded healers: the significance of personal histories

An important element in this research inquiry was the importance of each therapist's personal history in their decision to become therapists, and in which tradition they trained. In light of some of the better known therapists, many of whose concepts we use to inform our work, this is perhaps worthy of deeper, and more personal consideration. Like the Greek centaur god, Cheiron, they may have been able to heal others while finding it impossible to help themselves. Cheiron, in the end, begged to forfeit his immortality in order to die and escape his suffering (Graves, 1955, p. 55).

Rogers (1957, 1959) argued that congruence, empathy and unconditional positive regard were the 'necessary and sufficient' conditions for therapeutic change. In my view, he underestimated the impact of the therapist's unconscious personal process on the work. It is not enough simply to know or be congruent of your internal process, but to understand the implications and the possible unconscious motivations that have drawn you to the work in the first place.

Rogers was honest in his need for intimacy in the therapeutic encounter, something with which he apparently struggled in his personal life (1990, p. 47). Clearly, Rogers was a powerful therapist, deeply empathic, accepting and authentic in his approach to the world, his public persona reflecting the integrity of his private life. Though not without difficulties, his 'guru' status did not hide a man removed from the message he preached. Did he, however, need to be liked? Working with the transference demands that we accept feelings of hatred or anger from our clients, projections from their history played out in the room in order to 'work through' in the 'here-and-now' the trauma in their past. Rogers did not deny that transference existed, but he did not 'work' with it, believing it was the existing relationship between the counsellor and client that mattered. Arguably, this avoided more uncomfortable feelings in the room and satisfied his need for intimacy, a deep sharing through his qualities of empathy and UPR (unconditional postive regard) extended to his clients.

I use this example of Rogers to illustrate the point that how we use ourselves as therapists will inevitably impact our clients. Other 'gurus' perhaps illustrate in more dramatic form the discrepancy between 'life' and the public persona, such as R.D. Laing (Barston, 1996; Gordon, 2009), Scott Peck (Jones, 2007) or Eric Berne (Jorgensen and Jorgensen, 1984). The list is actually endless, including Melanie Klein, Masoud Kahn, and even Fairburn who, while preaching the value of attachment and the destructive force of the 'bad object' (1994), sent his own son, Nicholas, to boarding school.

None of this made them 'bad' therapists, or at least not all of time, though arguably in the case of some of them, by today's standards they would be held to account for their actions. Most of them, in fact, even the most disturbed of them, R.D. Laing for instance, were deeply effective therapists, often expressing profound qualities of empathy and compassion for their clients and patients. As Jones says of Scott Peck,

> Peck's cross in the road, as in his own life, was that he could see what people needed to do and describe how to do it, but scarcely practised what he preached regarding his own needs because of his narcissism. He became totally self-centred. (2007, p. 152)

In the case of each of these gurus, more obvious to us because of their public persona, what was avoided, and what was focused on as a result of their own internal struggles and vulnerabilities? In all of the examples I have cited, Rogers excepted, there were destructive elements in their relationships with others in their family lives, and with clients and patients, including substance abuse and boundary violations. Most of us live quieter lives, outside the public domain and beyond the prurient scrutiny of others. Our vulnerabilities are played out behind closed doors, held close to our chests and sometimes not admitted even to ourselves.

What is it that we unconsciously hope for in our work? While Rogers admitted his own desire for intimacy, how many of us acknowledge our own historical longings? Alice, in her wish for children, was open in her admission that her work with patients replicated the family she longed for. Raymond, a psychoanalytic therapist whose childhood was devoid of maternal warmth, sits facing his patients, believing that it is in the contact and the 'relationship' that the possibility for healing exists.

Most of us are not gurus, we are simply working therapists and, on the basis of the forty interviews I carried out, most of us work with the best of intentions. The discrepancies between our private and professional lives are usually not so pronounced as those of many of the 'gurus' whose theories we follow, but we do have private lives, and they can interfere with our work. They can also, of course, prove a positive force, our most profound experiences providing us with the possibility of extending a deeper empathy and understanding to our clients as a result of our pain, both physical and psychological. As the therapists in the study showed, we are unconsciously guided to our choice of profession through the very experiences which may inhibit our work, while also providing us with the capacity to do the work. We are, in a way, 'boxed in', a catch-22 that both enables and inhibits us. As 'wounded healers' the challenge, then, becomes how to distinguish between satisfaction and gratification. And how do we tell the difference?

Behaviour: a reflection of pain

'Can you look at pain?,' an elderly novelist of some note asked me over lunch one day. He knew I wanted to be a writer.

'Yes,' I responded blithely. I was only eighteen years of age and completely in awe of my host.

Since then I have been reminded of his question repeatedly, over the years recognising that more often than not I simply want to look away. There are times when it is easier to judge than to consider and avoid aspects of myself reflected back in someone else's negative behaviour.

In every tradition there were therapists who seemed to me to have a great capacity for self-reflection and appreciation of their contribution to the work, be it positive or negative. There were also a few therapists about whom I have doubts about their possible ability to reflect very deeply, or consider their own process in relation to their work. And within each tradition there were also those therapists I believe who particularly turned their heads in shame at their own vulnerability, or who maintained a stance of some superiority in order to deny the possibility that they might not always be aware of their unconscious motives for doing the work they do, or the effect this might have to the detriment of their work with clients and patients.

It is easy to condemn a therapist we believe is not working appropriately, whether they are actually crossing ethical boundaries or simply not working within the frame of 'good practice', so struggling in their personal lives it is hard to imagine they are able to simply leave their addictions or compulsions, their depression or anxieties by the door. Of course they cannot.

Following interviews with several therapists – one in each tradition – I was deeply disturbed, and also outraged. I carried these therapists with me, speaking about the interviews and their impact on me in supervision for several weeks afterwards. How could he or she be working, I ranted. Couldn't they *see* how harmful their attitude was, both to themselves and their clients? Gradually I calmed down. Over the months, and after interviewing so many other therapists, I began to recognise that my criticism of them was in part a reflection of those aspects of myself I did not want to see. Those psychotherapists in my view contain elements of *every* therapist. It is as if they hold in their self-destructive force and their unacknowledged pain the denial that we all maintain at times. Despite their faults, their internal disturbance is as real as those of any of our clients and patients and I believe they deserve compassion. And they were brave too, in the end spilling the beans and exposing themselves to possible censure by allowing me to interview them. I also believe their taking part was an unconscious plea for help, which I was not able to provide.

I want, as both a researcher and as a practising psychotherapist, to turn away from these therapists, to deny that they have anything to do with me or the way I live my life and practice. But I know that I, too, have sometimes struggled with the resentment that I can no longer do just what I want, when I want to do it, because I have a commitment to my patients that I will be there for them each week at the same time. These may be momentary regrets, small pangs in a life that I feel is pretty full and wonderful, but they do creep in from time to time. As someone who was once rather fond of a stiff whisky, I no longer drink. But some nights that cup of mint tea, or when I am very 'stressed' and I make myself a tall carafe of strong, decaffeinated coffee, it seems pretty tame and dull. I'd kill for a whisky.

But I also believe that in all of us there are features of denial and naïveté, a wish that our behaviour is always straightforward and without unconscious motivations pulling us towards personal gratification at the expense of our clients. We would like, at times, to believe that we have unearthed all there is to unearth about ourselves and that we have tamed the unconscious beast within. Of course, this is impossible but it doesn't stop the wishing.

Elements of these struggling therapists, I believe, are in all of us. We can blame them, or condemn them, but we cannot deny them. If we do that, we deny the very aspects in them that also reside in us: our capacity to work in contradictions, to ignore what is obvious and to defend ourselves against the hard truth that we may sometimes need help. These psychotherapists should not be working, at least until they have sought help, but they also deserve the same compassion we extend to those we work with, and some acknowledgement that how they live their lives now is somehow rooted in how they were treated, or experienced life way back then. Like every therapist and client, they are a product of their histories. And, like so many therapists who took part in this research, they also began their careers with the notion that they wanted to help others. 'I decided that I was going to be a psychotherapist so that nobody else would ever have to feel this way,' said one of them. In so many ways, they are no different than the rest of us.

Job satisfaction over disenchantment

Not a single therapist in this study said they had experienced disenchantment with the work itself, although five therapists working within mental health services expressed unhappiness with the *system* within which they worked. Therapists in this study overtly expressed their 'love' of the work, usually without being asked specifically.

Why enter a profession if we are not going to gain personal satisfaction as a result? While it is important to recognise how our histories might inhibit our work with clients and patients, it is also clear that without a history of some texture we would not be equipped to work with others in their pain and desperation. Therapy can provide a three-dimensional quality to our lives and our view of our own history, particularly when perhaps our best defence against the unbearable pain of our childhood or traumatic events has been to 'flat line', to depress our affect and rationalise our thinking to the extent that we no longer have to 'feel' the experience. We park it in our memory, or beyond access in our unconscious and simply keep on going. We cope, as Winifred pointed out when speaking of her history and tackling her illness while working, and in order to cope, we may also be obliged to negate the experience out of mind and out of feeling, beyond conscious reach until the crisis has passed. What might not be conscious may still play out through transference and counter-transference and the enactment of aspects of our own history to derive soothing and gratification in our work, rather than simple satisfaction.

The role of history in our choice to become therapists

A telling aspect in the history of a quarter of therapists in this study was their *witnessing* of another's pain. Mark, as a child, tried desperately to alleviate his mother's grief and worry after the tragic death of his father, while Terry, as a teenager was forced to endure her brother's increasingly deteriorating mental state. Both these children grew up to be CBT therapists, helping their clients to manage their lives, to find solutions to current difficulties and unravel their irrational thoughts. They provide tools for survival in a world that for many of their clients may seem impossible to control. As these therapists pointed out, their history has given them a capacity to understand their clients' helplessness, and there is deep satisfaction for both of them in being able to provide for others what they could not find for themselves as children.

If therapists become therapists because of their histories, they also become the kinds of therapists they do as a result of how they perceived and coped with their difficulties as children. In this study, all ten CBT therapists spoke across the board of having to *manage* their difficulties, while those therapists who work at the psychoanalytic end of the spectrum all spoke of a need to *understand* what had happened to them in order to cope, and even survive. In between, for instance, Katy, an integrative therapist who works primarily within a Gestalt tradition, including body therapy and constellation work, reflected on her own need as a child to *physically* express herself through music and externalise her struggle by keeping precious a box into which she metaphorically split off so much of what was terrible in her life. In Katy's case, as a result of her history, she is able to work with deeply dissociated patients, helping them to let go of their somatic states and make sense of their experience within a systemic context.

Psychotherapists are often best at what they do as a result of their histories. They are enabled in their work through the tragedies of their childhoods. And there is often a deep and profound satisfaction in the healing they witness as a result of their work together. What heals their clients and patients is also healing for them (Casement, 1985).

Within this capacity to work with elements that replicate our history, there are also hazards. Marcia, a humanistic therapist, acknowledged in her interview that her capacity to work with deeply disturbed and violent criminals was a legacy of her having to cope with an abusive stepmother and a violent and alcoholic father. For her, the threat of violence is her 'comfort zone' and she struggles to cope with the 'calm, just comfortable, loving' her partner is able to offer.

Who else, but someone with Marcia's capacity to survive within such a threatening environment, could actually work within a high-security prison? She is clearly needed. However, does drama need to be attached in order for her to experience satisfaction from her work, physical indications of relief and self-expression, through tears perhaps or verbal expression? Might the more subtle indications of insight or profound change be missed if they are manifested simply through quiet reflection, or a changed attitude which results in modified behaviour?

This is not simply Marcia's dilemma, it is every therapist's. Hers may simply be more obvious as a result of the drama attached to such an environment. In every therapist there may be the capacity for working in a particular setting and in a particular way because of their history, and there will also be an incapacity, a struggle to work with its opposite. In Marcia's case, she can face the violence in her clients head on. In my own case, I struggle with 'deadness', the depressive state in others which echoes my own need to enliven my mother (Green, 1983). Sometimes I cannot distinguish between a truly depressive state and reflective withdrawal in my patients. I need to force myself at times not to work to enliven *for my own sake* rather than theirs. Like any therapist, I too want to derive satisfaction from the job I do, without falling into the perils of gratification at the expense of my clients.

The need for a coherent story

Those therapists in this study who had not had therapy, or who had experienced only short-term interventions, tended to be less coherent in their narrative, less specific and clear than those who had experienced longer-term therapy. Those therapists who had not had therapy, or had experienced very little compared with their colleagues, also looked sheepish when discussing whether or not they had attended therapy. There were clear signs of embarrassment, or 'shame', including shuffling their feet and avoiding eye contact with me (Nathanson, 1987). Two CBT therapists, neither of whom had experienced personal therapy, also expressed a direct wish that therapy be a requirement in training. Another therapist also stated that she 'should have' long-term therapy, but had only ever availed herself of very short-term interventions, primarily couples' counselling. She also suffers with chronic depression, and drug and alcohol dependency.

Conversely, this does not mean that everyone in the other traditions who had undergone therapy, sometimes extensively, were always able to reflect on their internal process in a meaningful way, at least with me. For instance, one therapist who could not recognise where his personal life might impact on others, though he could see it in colleagues, had experienced years of therapy and still occasionally took part in therapy workshops focusing on personal process. He was also dismissive of the therapists he had worked with, suggesting that they had misunderstood him, attributing transference issues to his responses that he did not believe were correct.

Whatever else therapy might offer it does, in most cases, appear to provide a coherence, or a narrative around which therapists are able to make sense of their own story. If they are able to make sense of themselves, at least to a degree, they may also be able to help their clients and patients make sense of their world.

Like actors who need to fill in their character's 'back story' in order to give authenticity to their performance, so do we need to know our own history, in the deepest sense, including an awareness that there are often times when we will be working from unconscious motivations, or in the humanistic terminology, out-of-awareness. Like with an actor, the audience may not know the back story any more than our clients and patients need to know ours, but *we* need to know it in order to ensure integrity in our role as psychotherapists.

Any therapist is at a disadvantage if they do not understand their own 'back story'. I agree with Jones (1997), that psychotherapy is warranted for CBT therapists in order to mitigate the stress of working 'day after day with depressed patients, endlessly wrestling with complex logical but irrational negative thoughts' (p. 148). I also believe that CBT therapists would benefit from a deeper process of therapy in order to put their experience and their own negative thinking within a deeper historical context. Therapists of every persuasion need to be 'ahead' of their clients in personal development, in making sense of their own narrative. It is difficult enough for any therapist, of any tradition and after years of effective therapy, to sometimes distinguish between the client's needs and their own, let alone a therapist without the advantage of therapy and an understanding of the complexities of their own story and how that might play out in the therapy room (Mann, 1997; Mann and Cunningham, 2008).

My argument here is not that CBT therapy is a 'lesser breed'. Having begun this study with a bias favouring the other traditions, I have emerged the other end with a far greater appreciation of the effort, effectiveness and integrity of the therapists working within CBT. But I also noticed their struggle at times to define themselves within their history, to grapple with a coherent narrative, particularly around trauma. And I wonder how this affects their work with clients, many of whom will be struggling with their own stories through debilitating defences such as depression and self-defeating compulsions.

But therapists who have had therapy in the past may need to consider further why they do not return to therapy in times of 'trouble' and distress and to consider why they do not trust therapists other than themselves. Why is there such 'shame' in our need for another? We are 'relationship seeking beings' (Fairbairn, 1994), and therapy is one means through which we can explore this need, or our resistance to it. In my view, when we experience an aversion to something, a qualitative resistance that is visceral, but intellectually rationalised, it is wise to consider whether this might be the product of unconscious motivations and unacknowledged defensiveness. Perhaps it is the same mechanism that functions around clinical supervision. If there is a resistance, or a disinclination to raise an issue in supervision, there is usually a very good reason why it should be raised in discussion. It is through the very discomfort that some understanding may be achieved, and we find some means of working through the dilemma or temptation, the breaking of a professional boundary being the most obvious.

Managing things differently: the struggle to seek help

The therapeutic community is a remarkably small one, particularly within each of the traditions. To my surprise several therapists in Australia, chosen at random and who had not known me previously, were familiar with some of the trainers at the institute in the UK where I have done much of my training. In Canada, too, there were professional exchanges with colleagues in the UK. This illustrates some of the difficulties of ensuring privacy, particularly within the even smaller therapeutic communities of any given area.

Geography may play a part in our resistance to seeking out therapy, making it almost impossible to find a therapist in the area with whom we are not on personal or professional terms. And if we do not know them specifically, they will certainly be on familiar terms with someone we know, and may even be in supervision with them, or in a peer supervision group. The boundaries blur. For a number of therapists who took part in this research, they are also well-known and respected teachers of counselling and psychotherapy, one therapist pointing out that he had taught 'most of the therapists in this town'. To whom might he go for therapy?

However, this may only be a problem if we are ashamed of our vulnerability. Why would we not trust in the therapist's capacity to maintain confidentiality? In my experience, most therapists say that they certainly trust their own capacity to hold the boundary. One therapist in this study, however, went one further, stating that the only therapist he actually trusted was himself. In not trusting others, has he simply made vocal what others in the profession just keep to themselves, *If only I could be my therapist!* Once again, this is a narcissistic position, believing that the only really trustworthy therapist is one's self.

But narcissism is simply the flip side of confidence, where shame actually resides (Symington, 1993). We may rationalise our struggle to find appropriate therapy, but we may also be defending ourselves against the possibility of revealing ourselves and, as a consequence, facing our own fallibility in the very area where our credentials claim we are an expert, the psychological well-being of others.

As I have already stated, there are different styles of learning for each of the four traditions in which the therapists I interviewed for this research trained. For CBT therapists, therapy during training is not mandated, although only two therapists working in this area who took part in this study had never had therapy. Most CBT therapists have experienced at least a short intervention within their own tradition, and just under half of them in this research study had attended therapy in traditions other than the one in which they trained. This was also true for therapists in the other three traditions, at least two of whom mentioned making use of CBT, particularly to alleviate the symptoms of depression.

Incidence of depression across the four traditions

Of the forty therapists I interviewed for the formal aspect of this study, twenty-two admitted having experienced what they termed 'depression' during the time they have been working as psychotherapists.

Depression, according to the therapists in the study, and in every tradition, stressed the importance of shared experience as a means for developing deeper connections with their clients and patients. Therapists appear to be able to work very often while still in a depressive state, including while coping with grief and loss. All the therapists in this study who had continued working during these periods spoke of work as a 'refuge' from the despair they felt outside the therapy room.

While I do not doubt that their suffering opened them up to their clients' anguish, I wonder at the impact this may have had on them, not necessarily always positive. If we believe, as nearly all of the therapists in this study did, that our personal lives affect our work, *without our patients being told*, then surely they will have picked up *our* need for solace, if only unconsciously. For the client who is eager to please, for instance, or who was forced in childhood to become a caretaker, this could prove very difficult, particularly if the therapist is so consumed with their own internal struggle that the care of the patient is unconsciously welcome. Under these circumstances, how attuned to the transference and counter-transference of such an enactment will we be? What might the patient bring, or not bring, in order to care for his therapist? What might not be 'worked through' so much as enacted, the dead weight of a patient's history played out once again without the benefit of insight and resolution, simply because it might be too painful for us, the therapist.

'Anxiety' is a more obvious interference with the work, with symptoms of distraction and pre-occupation at the core. Work may sometimes provide an escape from anxiety, but by its very nature may not allow for deep contact or appropriate 'tuning in' to our clients and patients. Anxiety may mean we simply stay on the surface of things. Why on earth would we want to delve more deeply into another's core distress while we are having trouble enough dealing with our own? Anxiety is visceral and could be said to be our best defence against depression or 'death' (Freud, 1995a). If this is so, there will be an unconscious resistance to delving too deeply into a patient's depressive state, to work through the internal death or sorrow at the heart of someone else's internal world. We will unconsciously avoid, perhaps, that which will remind us too deeply of what we, ourselves, are trying to ignore.

'Depression' can clearly open us up to the intense pain of another's experience, though perhaps the benefits of a therapist's personal struggle might be better used following recovery. There may not be simply a 'right' way to manage, but it does beg the question; when are we equipped to work during periods of depression, and when are we not? Donald's depression was so severe that he could not work and when, during his last bout of illness his psychiatrist suggested that he take an additional month off to recover, he was greatly relieved.

There are no right answers, each therapist being responsible for considering when they are able, or not, to work. But that decision is often cluttered with internal messages concerning our patients' 'need' for us, our responsibilities to the job and our commitment to those we work with. We may also have internal messages that tell us we 'must' work through difficult times, or we may have more practical concerns, like rent and mortgages and our children's education. We may also not want to be left alone with ourselves during difficult times, away from work and the opportunity of relief from our distress.

Siobhan spoke powerfully of her capacity to sit with her patients in deep pain following the death of her husband. She said that she was 'often in a worse state' than her patients. She was in so much pain, she claimed, that she had a greater 'capacity' for containing other people's suffering. She also delineated between pain and anxiety, her ability to stay with the former, rather than the latter during the early stages of her widowhood.

But anxiety, the pre-occupation with our own experience, drives us apart. No longer are we able to use our internal experience as a map to explore the internal world of others, but we are distracted, unable to connect, sometimes not even with our deeper selves. As Carmen expressed, her physical pain enabled her to understand others, but in moments of acute physical suffering, she was not, in her words, 'fully present'. In Wallace's case, his pre-occupation with external noises was a clue to his internal distress and pre-occupation with his own pain, despite his wish to 'brush' it off.

Hanford, too, was articulate in his description of his anxiety, and the impact this had on his work with clients. He could not attend to them appropriately, and began to consider his clinical work a 'burden'. In his case, he was able to take two extended periods of leave in order to recover.

Hanford and Siobhan are two sides of the coin; therapists in this study named depression as a vehicle for developing deeper empathy and understanding towards their clients and patients, while anxiety proved a detriment to their work.

This is also interesting because therapists could name depression as ultimately positive in their development as therapists, but anxiety was identified by only a few, although in their description of events, this became obvious; for instance, therapists when speaking of outside preoccupations, such as Ben when discussing his partner's illness, or Katy having to deal with her father's psychosis. Pauline, in her anxiety concerning her partner's and her mother's deteriorating mental state, was forced to take a whole year off in order to cope and recover from the stress of that period.

Managing the crisis differently

For many years I worked in a newsroom, a hotbed of startling intelligence and cynicism. Terrible jokes following a catastrophe were rampant, a means of discharging anxiety and dealing with unbearable human suffering. There is just so much that any one human being can take. Regardless of the complexity of our own histories, we will be exposed to unfamiliar aspects of pain and suffering within the therapy room beyond which most of us could never have previously imagined. Nothing can prepare us. Like journalists in the field of war, a theoretical understanding of human despair and cruelty is simply not enough. Fergal Keane, a journalist with the BBC and an experienced war correspondent was in Rwanda during the time of the massacres.

> I had an intellectual understanding of what the word massacre meant from reading books. But books don't smell. Books don't rot. Books don't lie in stagnant pools. Books don't leach into the earth the way those bodies did. They can't tell you about it. Nothing can tell you about it except the experience of going there and seeing it.
>
> (Keane, 2001)[1]

As psychotherapists we are also on the 'frontline' of our patients' experiences and trauma, often having to bear witness to the most terrible aspects of the human condition. And there is only so much we can take.

When we begin to make jokes about our patients, to dread seeing them or want to veer away from the more difficult aspects of their experience that cause us pain, anger or hatred, we know we are in trouble. When we are sarcastic about a patient's presentation, about their behaviour or manner of relating to others, these are all symptoms of overload, the potential for 'burn out'.

Crucially, when the therapists in this study were asked whether they would manage their personal crisis differently in the future, the most common regret was that they had not taken 'more time off'. As Ben pointed out, however, this is not always easy and those therapists working in private practice are particularly vulnerable to financial concerns. Hanford, although working within the medical health system and given paid leave, articulated a professional concern; he believes he ended with his patients too suddenly. If we hang on too long before taking time out, this may be inevitable in many cases. A slower withdrawal at the early signs of symptoms may mean a faster recovery and a less traumatic ending for our clients and patients. Hanford now has a plan in place, in consultation with his supervisor, to ensure that his ending with patients will be less abrupt in the future should he become ill again.

The role of supervision in managing crisis

Clinical supervision is a critical component in the work we do. It is, for many of us, an insurance policy, ensuring that we maintain our integrity as psychotherapists and the ethical boundaries which provide our patients and clients with containment within the clinical setting.

Virtually all the therapists in this study availed themselves of regular supervision, and for most of them it is a professional requirement. However, not everyone attends individual supervision. Five therapists in this study stated that they made use of peer supervision instead, rather than a paid, formal relationship with a supervisor, and another therapist said her personal therapy, after many years, had now evolved into a form of supervision.

How effective supervision is for any therapist depends on what they bring, what they reveal of themselves through their counter-transferential responses to their clients and patients, or what they reveal concerning the state of their personal lives and psychological state at the moment. The supervisor, too, must be in a healthy state of psychological health to ensure good supervision.

Two therapists stated that they relied on their supervisors to 'inform' them when they might be in an 'unfit' state to practice. This is very different from using supervision, as Hanford does, to ensure that if in an unfit state, he works ethically and compassionately towards an ending with his clients if he finds himself once again having to close his practice.

What is the role of the supervisor, at least in the mind of the supervisee? Supervisors cannot be expected to see beyond what is presented, although often there is a 'sense' that a counsellor or psychotherapist is working from an unconscious, parallel position in their work with a client. If there is an open process of exploration and discovery between them, much of what might be enacted in the therapy room is able to come to light. However, if there is a parallel process, an unconscious enactment between the supervisor and supervisee, this can prove difficult, particularly if there is shame on the part of the therapist to reveal their level of distress or vulnerability to their supervisor. These are wheels within wheels perhaps, but a therapist who relies on their supervisor to determine whether or not they are fit to work may also have a responsibility to let them know when they are not well enough to work. And letting them know may demand exposure, a painful enough process at times to acknowledge to oneself, let alone to a supervisor. There is a further paradox; if a therapist is willing to reveal the extent of his or her vulnerability to the supervisor, they may already be equipped to determine their own way forward. Like Donald, however, they may need 'permission' to take a break, a reassuring nod that a longer period away is not only 'okay', but essential.

And, of course, there may be a deeper conflict – the need to work for financial reasons against the argument that the therapist could well do with a break. This tension was overtly expressed by nearly a quarter of the therapists participating in this study. How can a supervisor help a therapist through a difficult period when their taking a break might result in devastating consequences? And working, of course, can mean a distraction from personal worries.

Not every therapist who is struggling may need to take a break, but simply to work with additional caution, and an additional focus on what they might be avoiding or gravitating towards as a result of their personal distress. How is their history impacting their work, what is familiar in their feelings towards their clients, or a particular patient, and what additional supervision do they need to avail themselves of? What are they bringing to supervision, and what are they not? What would they prefer to remain hidden, and what are they bringing that is more likely to show them in a good light within supervision? How do they feel in relation to their work at the moment? Do they dread working with clients, or a particular patient, and why?

A supervisor is not a mind reader or a magician, but another professional likely doing the best they can for their supervisee. Like our own work with clients, the job demands something from those we work with. No therapist can work without the conscious willingness of his or her patients, even if there is inevitably an unconscious pull to resist change. We are no different in our relationships with our supervisors. We have to work with them, and not expect more than they can reasonably provide. Just as we ask of our patients and clients that they work through their trauma within the safety of the clinical setting, so do we also need to admit and establish a narrative around our own internal difficulties. We are no different than those we work with, entirely human.

Like those we seek to treat, every therapist has a personal life, and sometimes it is complicated. Therapists have children, get divorced, become ill, and find joy in their work. They need to pay their mortgages, educate their kids and all the while keep up their professional profiles. Therapists' stories are both endless and timeless and connect them most deeply with those they meet in the therapy room. Empathy is a product of our shared histories and experience, but anxiety is a current that keeps us apart from those we work with.

From the beginning ...

Who trains as a therapist, and why? Whether it is a diploma counselling course, or a post-graduate psychotherapy training programme, selection for candidate training is crucial.

As anyone who has ever worked as a trainer will tell you, even unlikely candidates can often blossom during their years of training, using therapy and the personal process aspects of the course to develop and understand their internal world. They do, quite clearly, change before our eyes and develop into compassionate and insightful practitioners, or so we believe.

Most training programmes stress the need for self-development and insight, even those which do not mandate personal therapy. But how can we ensure that this is taken up, and the practitioner who emerges cannot simply just talk a good game, but is also personally invested in developing his or her internal world? Most therapists do work in the service of others, but *all* of them also work in the service of themselves.

Why is it that so many therapists feel personal shame at revealing their vulnerabilities once they are past qualifying? Certainly in my own training it was stressed that therapy may be helpful once past the qualifying post. It was even stressed that we had an obligation to return to therapy if life became difficult or we encountered something in our work that evoked earlier trauma in ourselves. However, as a result of this study, my suspicion is that the shame resides in the fact that life does become difficult at times, or that we cannot manage. Earlier trauma is, in one way or another, supposed to have been 'worked through' during the early years of therapy, or in the case of many CBT therapists, managed with the tools of their trade. When they are not, they feel a failure of some sort. If we cannot keep ourselves psychologically healthy, how can we promote the psychological health of others? The best means of dealing with this may be to simply deny that we need help, cling to our narcissistic raft and hope that we can endure until the storm passes.

Perhaps training programmes need to re-consider how the idea of psychological insight and recovery from trauma might be promoted. I believe we need to stress that it is not *if* we encounter difficulties in our work and in life, but rather *when* we encounter them. And we also need to lay out a series of strategies that therapists can consider in advance. This will not, of course, enable us to deal with every contingency, but it may prepare us, at the very least, to consider how crisis might be managed.

As a community we need to give thought to how we support one another in the struggles of our everyday lives, and we need to consider how our personal experience can both enable and inhibit our work with clients and patients. We need to examine how we use supervision to enable us to work appropriately and provide us with containment, and as trainers we need to reflect on how we encourage our students to view therapy as a tool for their future work with clients and therapists, not so much as 'homework' but as part of developing a deeper understanding of ourselves which we can then extent to our clients and patients. We need to diffuse the notion that therapy following our qualifying is a matter of shame that we cannot cope, but rather indicative of a personal strength that we are willing to reach out to others for help.

We are all products of our histories, and we all function from unconscious motivations at times, particularly concerning our choice of profession. How do we ensure that how we work within the therapy room is to the *benefit* of our clients and not purely for personal gratification at the *expense* of our clients and patients? Vulnerability and pain are not the enemy. Providing they are owned and acknowledged, respected for the weight and texture they give to our lives, they will be the very tools through which we do our best work.

Note

1 http://www.pbs.org/wgbh/pages/frontline/shows/ghosts/interviews/keane.html

References

Adams, M. (2008), 'Abandonment: Enactments from the Patient's Sadism and the Therapist's Collusion'. In D. Mann and V. Cunningham (eds), *The Past in the Present: Therapy Enactment and the Return of Trauma*. London: Routledge.

Adams, P. (2003), *Summer of the Heart: Saving Alexandre*. Toronto: Macfarlane Walter & Ross.

Akeret, R. U. (1995), *The Man Who Loved a Polar Bear*. London: Penguin Books.

Bager-Charleson, S. (2010), *Why Therapists Choose to Become Therapists*. London: Karnac Books.

Barston, D. (1996), *The Wing of Madness: The Life and Work of RD Laing*. Cambridge, MA: Harvard University Press.

Basescu, C. (2001), 'The Ongoing, Mostly Happy "Crisis" of Parenthood and Its Effect on the Therapist's Clincal Work'. In B. Gerson (ed.), *The Therapist as a Person*. Burlingame, CA: Analytic Press.

BBC (2012), 'Ugandan Asians', *The Reunion* BBC Radio 4 radio broadcast (45 minutes), August 31, Whistledown Production.

Beckett, S. (1958), *Endgame*. New York: Grove Press.

Berne, E. (1964), *Games People Play: The Basic Handbook for Transactional Analysis*. New York: Ballantine.

Bernier, T. and Kearns, A. (2007), 'Where There's Smoke There's Fire'. In A. Kearns (ed.), *The Mirror Crack'd* (pp. 105–124). London: Karnac.

Beskind, H., Bartels, S. J. and Brooks, M. (1993), 'Practical and Theoretical Dilemmas of Dynamic Psychotherapy in a Small Community'. In J. H. Gold and J. C. Nemiah (eds), *Beyond Transference*. Washington, DC: American Psychiatric Press.

Bird, L. (1999), *The Fundamental Facts*. London: Mental Health Foundation.

Bollas, C. (1987), *The Shadow of the Object*. London: Free Association Books.

Bonnici, P. (2011), 'Who Am I If Not a Mother? Separating Womanhood from Motherhood: A Phenomenological Exploration of the Identity of Childfree Women', *SPCP*. London: Regents College.

Boorman, J. (1972), *Deliverance* (109 minutes). Burbank, CA: Warner Brothers, Elmer Enterprises.

Boseley, S. (2012), 'Work Stress Can Raise Risk of Heart Attack by 23%, Study Finds'. *The Guardian*, September 14.

Bowlby, J. (1991), *Attachment and Loss Volume 1*. London: Penguin.

Breuer, J. and Freud, S. (1895), 'Studies On Hysteria'. (Standard ed.,Vol. 2): London: Hogarth Press.

Brown, C. (2000), *Manchild in the Promised Land*. New York: Touchstone.

Bugental, J. F. T. (1992), *The Art of Psychotherapy*. New York: W.W. Norton.

Campbell, A. (2008), *All in the Mind*. London: Hutchinson.

Carroll, M. (1996), *Counselling Supervision*. London: Cassell.

Casement, P. (1985), *On Learning from the Patient*. London: Routledge.

Casement, P. (1990), *Further Learning from the Patient*. London: Routledge.

Charles, S. C. and Kennedy, E. (1985), *Defendant*. New York: The Free Press.

Chasen, B. (2001), 'Death of a Psychoanalyst's Child'. In B. Gerson (ed.), *The Therapist as a Person* (pp. 3–20). Burlingame, CA: Analytic Press.

Coles, R. (1989), *The Call of Stories*. Boston, MA: Houghton Mifflin.

Cray, C. and Cray, M. (1977), 'Stresses and Rewards within the Psychiatrist's Family'. *American Journal of Psychoanalysis, 37,* 337–341.

Cullington-Roberts, D. (2004), 'The Psychotherapist's Miscarriage and Pregnancy as an Obstacle to Containment'. *Psychoanalytic Psychotherapy, 18,* 99–110.

de Zulueta, F. (1993), *From Pain to Violence*. London: Whurr.

Duffell, N. (2000), *The Making of Them*. London: Lone Arrow Press.

Etchegoyen, A. (1993), 'The Analyst's Pregnancy and its Consequences on the Work'. *International Journal of Psychoanalysis, 74,* 141–149.

Eysenck, H. J. (ed.) (1976), *Case Studies in Behaviour Therapy*. London: Routledge.

Fairbairn, W. R. D. (1994), *Psychoanalytic Studies of the Personality*. London: Routledge.

Faulkner, W. (1951), *Requiem for a Nun*. New York: Random House.

Ferrell, R. B. and Price, T. R. P. (1993), 'Effects of Malpractice Suits on Physicians'. In J. H. Gold and J. C. Nemiah (eds), *Beyond Transference*. Washington, DC: American Psychiatric Press.

Fitzgerald, F. S. (1933), *Tender is the Night*. New York: Scribner.

Frankl, V. (1959), *Man's Search for Meaning*. New York: Washington Square Press.

Freud, S. (1913), 'On Beginning the Treatment (Further Recommendations on the Technique of Psycho Analysis I)' (Standard ed., Vol 2, 121–144). London: Hogarth Press.

Freud, S. (1915), *The Unconscious*. (Standard edition, Vol. 8) London: Hogarth Press.

Freud, S. (1917), 'Mourning and Melancholia' (Standard ed., Vol. 14) London: Hogarth Press.

Freud, S. (1937), *Analysis Terminable and Interminable*. (Standard ed., Vol. 23) London: Hogarth Press.

Freud, S. (1995a), 'Mourning and Melancholia'. In P. Gay (ed.), *The Freud Reader* (pp. 584–589). London: Vintage.

Freud, S. (1995b), 'On Beginning the Treatment'. In P. Gay (ed.), *The Freud Reader* (pp. 363–378). London: Vintage.

Freudenburger, H. J. (1986), 'Chemical Abuse Among Psychologists: Symptoms, Causes and Treatment Issues'. In R. R. Kilburg, P. E. Nathan and R. W. Thoreson (eds), *Professionals in Distress: Issues, Syndromes and Solutions in Psychology*. Washington, DC: American Psychological Association.

Freudenberger, H. J. and Robbins, A. (1979), 'The Hazards of Being a Therapist'. *Psychoanalytic Review*, 66, 275–296.

Gawande, A. (2003), *Complications: A Surgeon's Notes on an Imperfect Science*. London: Profile Books.

Geller, J. D., Norcross, J. C. and Orlinsky, D. E. (eds) (2005), *The Psychotherapist's Own Psychotherapy*. New York: Oxford University Press.

Gerhardt, S. (2004), *Why Love Matters*. London: Routledge.

Gilbert, M. C. and Evans, K. (2000), *Psychotherapy Supervision*. Buckingham: Open University.

Gold, J. H. and Nemiah, J. C. (eds) (1993), *Beyond Transference*. Washington, DC: American Psychiatric Press.

Golden, V. and Farber, B. A. (1998), 'Therapists as Parents: Is It Good for the Children'. *Professional Psychology: Research and Practice*, 29 (2), 135–139.

Gordon, P. (2009), 'RD Laing in Context'. *The Psychotherapist*, Autumn (43), 10–12.

Gottlieb, L. (2012), 'What Brand Is Your Therapist?' *New York Times*, November 23.

Graves, R. (1955), *The Greek Myths*. London: Penguin.

Green, A. (1983), 'The Dead Mother', *On Private Madness* (pp. 142–173). London: Hogarth (1986).

Greenberger, D. and Padesky, C. A. (1995), *Mind Over Mood*. New York: Guilford Press.

Guggenbuhl-Craig, A. (1971), *Power in the Helping Professions*. Irving, TX: Spring Publications.

Guntrip, H. (1992), *Schizoid Phenomena, Object Relations and the Self*. London: Karnac.

Guy, J. D. (1987), *The Personal Life of the Psychotherapist*. New York: John Wiley & Sons.

Harrington, M. (1998), *The Other America: Poverty in the United States*. New York: Simon & Schuster.

Jacobs, M. (1995), *D.W. Winnicott*. London: Sage.

Jamison, K. R. (1996), *An Unquiet Mind*. London: Picador.

Johansen, K. H. (1993), 'Countertransference and Divorce of the Therapist'. In J. H. Gold and J. C. Nemiah (eds), *Beyond Transference* (pp. 87–108). Washington, DC: American Psychiatric Press.

Jones, A. (2007), *The Road He Travelled*. London: Random House.

Jones, D. (1997), 'Stresses in Cognitive Behavioural Psychotherapists'. In V. P. Varma (ed.), *Stress in Psychotherapists*. London: Routledge.

Jorgensen, E. W. and Jorgensen, H. I. (1984), *Eric Berne: Master Gamesman*. New York: Grove Press.

Kahn, M. (2000), *Between Therapist and Client*. (revised edn). New York: W.H. Freeman.

Katzenbach, J. (2002), *The Analyst*. London: Corgi Books.

Keane, F. (2001), *Ghosts of Rwanda*, available online at http://www.pbs.org/wgbh/pages/frontline/shows/ghosts/interviews/keane.html. Last accessed Jan 23, 2013.

Kearns, A. (2007), *The Mirror Crack'd*. London: Karnac.

Khan, M. R. (1964), 'Ego-distortion, Cumulative Trauma and the Role of Reconstruction in the Analytic Situation'. *International Journal of Psychoanalysis*, 45, 272–279.

Kivimäki, M. *et al.* (2012), 'Job Strain as a Risk Factor for Coronary Heart Disease: a Collaborative meta-analysis of individual participant data'. *The Lancet*, October 27, 380 (9852), 1491–1497, doi: 10.1016/S0140-6736(12)60994-5.

Kleespies, P. M., Orden, K. A. V., Bongar, B., Bridgeman, D., Bufka, L. F., Galper, D. I., Hillbrand, M. and Yufit, R. I. (2011), 'Psychologist Suicide: Incidence, Impact, and Suggestions for Prevention, Intervention, and Postvention'. *Professional Psychology: Research and Practice*, 42 (3), 244-251.

Klein, M. (1946 [1984]), 'Notes on Some Schizoid Mechanisms'. In J. Mitchell (ed.), *The Selected Melanie Klein*. New York: Free Press.

Klein, M. (1984), *Envy and Gratitude, and Other works 1946–1963*. London: Hogarth Press

Kottler, J. A. (2010), *On Being a Therapist*. San Francisco, CA: Jossey-Bass.

Kubler-Ross, E. (1969), *On Death and Dying*. New York: Macmillan.

Laing, A. (2006), *R.D. Laing, A Life*. Stroud: Sutton Publishing.

Lasky, R. (1990), 'Catastrophic Illness in the Analyst and the Analyst's Emotional Reactions to It'. *International Journal of Psychoanalysis*, 71, 455–473.

Leader, D. (2008), *The New Black: Mourning, Melancholia and Depression*. London: Hamish Hamilton.

LeDoux, J. (1998), *The Emotional Brain*. London: Weidenfeld and Nicholson.

Maeder, T. (1990), *Children of Psychiatrists and Other Psychotherapists*. New York: Harper and Row.

Mair, K. (1994), 'The Myth of Therapist Expertise'. In W. Dryden and C. Feltham (eds), *Psychotherapy and its Discontents*. Buckingham: Open University Press.

Mann, D. (1997), *Psychotherapy: An Erotic Relationship, Transference and Countertransference Passions*. London: Routledge.

Mann, D. and Cunningham, V. (eds) (2008), *The Past in the Present: Therapy Enactment and the Return of Trauma*. London: Routledge.

Maroda, K. J. (2004), *The Power of Counter-Transference*. Hillsdale, NJ: Analytic Press.

Martin, P. (1997), *The Sickening Mind*. London: Harper Collins.

Masefield, J. (1902), 'Sea Fever', *Salt-water Poems and Ballads*. New York: Macmillan.

Maslach, C. (1986), 'Stress, Burnout and Workaholism'. In R. R. Kilburg, P. E. Nathan and R. W. Thoreson (eds), *Professionals in Distress; Issues, Syndromes and Solutions in Psychology*. Washington, DC: American Psychological Association.

Masson, J. (1989), *Against Therapy*. London: Harper Collins.

Masson, J. M. (1993), *My Father's Guru*. New York: Pocket Books.

McGrath, P. (2008), *Trauma*. London: Bloomsbury.

Mollon, P. (1997), 'Supervision as a Space for Thinking'. In G. Shipton (ed.), *Supervision of Psychotherapy and Counselling*. Buckingham: Open University.

Moustakas, C. E. (1961), *Loneliness*. New York: Prentice Hall Press.

Moustakas, C. E. (1990), *Heuristic Research*. Newbury Park, CA: Sage Publications.

Mowrer, O. H. (1939), 'A Stimulus–Response Analysis of Anxiety and Its Role as a Reinforcing Agent'. *Psychology Review*, (46), 553–565.

Murdin, L. (2012), *How Money Talks*. London: Karnac.

Nathanson, D. L. (1987), *The Many Faces of Shame*. New York: Guilford Press.

Norcross, J. C. and Guy, J. D. (2007), *Leaving it at the Office: A Guide to Psychotherapist Self-Care*. New York: Guildford Press.

Office for National Statistics (2000), 'Psychiatric Morbidity Among Adults in Private Households in Great Britain'. London: Office for National Statistics.

Office for National Statistics (2012), 'Suicide Rates in the United Kingdom, 2006 to 2010'. London: Office for National Statistics.

Peck, M. S. (1978), *The Road Less Travelled*. New York: Simon and Schuster.

Pizer, B. (1998), 'Breast Cancer in the Analyst'. In L. Aron and F. Anderson (eds), *Relational Perspectives on the Body*. London: Routledge.

Pope, K. S. and Tabachnick, B. G. (1994), 'A National Survey of Psychologists' Experiences, Problems and Beliefs'. *Professional Psychology: Research and Practice*, 25, 247–258.

Racker, H. (1968), *Transference and Countertransference*. London: Karnac.

Ragen, T. (2009), *The Consulting Room and Beyond*. New York: Routledge.

Raskin, N. J. (1978), 'Becoming – A Therapist, A Person, A Partner, A Parent, A … ' *Psychotherapy: Theory, Research and Practice,* 15 (4)*,* 362–370.

Renn, P. (2012), *The Silent Past and the Invisible Present: Memory, Trauma, and Representation in Psychotherapy*. London: Routledge.

Rizq, R. (2012), 'The Ghost in the Machine: IAPT and Organisational Melancholia'. *British Journal of Psychotherapy,* 28 (3)*,* 319–335.

Rogers, C. (1957), 'The Necessary and Sufficient Conditions of Therapeutic Personality Change'. *Journal of Consulting Psychology,* 21 (2)*,* 95–103.

Rogers, C. (1959), 'A Theory of Therapy, Personality, and Interpersonal Relationships, As Developed in the Client-Centred Framework'. In S. Koch (ed.), *Psychology, A Study of Science* (pp. 184–256). New York: McGraw Hill.

Rogers, C. (1967), *On Becoming a Person*. London: Constable.

Rogers, C. (1990), *The Carl Rogers Reader*. London: Constable.

Ronnestad, M. H. and Orlinsky, D. E. (2009), 'Clinical Implications: Training, Supervision and Practice'. In D. E. Orlinsky and M. H. Ronnestad (eds), *How Psychotherapists Develop*. Washington, DC: American Psychological Association.

Roosevelt, F. D. (1933), T*he Public Papers of Franklin D. Roosevelt, Volume Two: The Year of Crisis*, S. Rosenman (ed.), Vol. Two, pp. 11–16. Ann Arbor, MI: University of Michigan Press.

Rutter, P. (1989), *Sex in the Forbidden Zone*. New York: Fawcett Columbine.

Schlachet, P. J. (2001), 'When the Therapist Divorces'. In B. Gerson (ed.), *The Therapist as a Person* (pp. 141–158). Burlingame, CA: Analytic Press.

Secunda, V. (1997), *When Madness Comes Home*. New York: Hyperion.

Sedgwick, D. (1994), *The Wounded Healer*. London: Routledge.

Solomon, A. (2001), *The Noonday Demon*. London: Chatto and Windus.

Stadien, M. (2010), 'Five Minutes With: Alain de Botton', BBC Radio 4 broadcast, November 20. Available online at http://www.bbc.co.uk/news/entertainment-arts-11799527.

Stern, D. N. (1985), *The Interpersonal World of the Infant*. New York: Basic Books.

Stobart, G. (2008), *Testing Times: The Uses and Abuses of Assessment*. London: Routledge.

Storr, A. (1990), *The Art of Psychotherapy*. (second edn). Oxford: Butterworth-Heinemann.

Styron, W. (1990), *Darkness Visible*. New York: Random House.

Sussman, M. (2007), *A Curious Calling*. Lanham, MD: Aronson.

Symington, N. (1993), *Narcissism: A New Theory*. London: Karnac.

Watkins, S. (2012), 'The Guinea Pig Club'. York: York Theatre Royal & Vroom Productions.

Winnicott, D. W. (1947), 'Hate in the Countertransference', *Through Pediatrics to Psychanalysis*. London: Karnac.

Winnicott, D. W. (1990 [1963]), 'Communicating and Not Communicating Leading to a Study of Certain Opposites', *The Maturational Processess and the Facilitating Environment* (pp. 179-192). London: Karnac.

Yalom, I. (1980), *Existential Psychotherapy*. New York: Basic Books.

Yalom, I. (1995), *The Theory and Practice of Group Psychotherapy*. New York: Basic Books. Yalom, I. (1996), *Lying on the Couch*. New York: Basic Books.

Yalom, I. (2002), *The Gift of Therapy*. London: Piatkus.

Index